Living:
We've Just Begun

Douglas Cooper

Pacific Press Publishing Association
Mountain View, California
Oshawa, Ontario

Library of Congress Cataloging in Publication Data
Cooper, Douglas.
Living—we've just begun.
(Redwood)
Includes bibliographical references.
1. Mystical union. 2. Christian life—Seventh-Day Adventist authors. I. Title.
BT769.C66 1983 248.4'8673 82-14242
ISBN 0-8163-0505-6

Contents

1
To Enter Within the Veil

Having therefore, brethren, boldness to enter into the holiest by the blood of Jesus, by a new and living way, which he hath consecrated for us, through the veil. Hebrews 10:19, 20.

Moment of mystery. There are those occasions when men's carefully conceived concepts crumble. The usual order of things, assumed to be unchangeable, changes. An unexplainable, unexpected force intervenes in time and space. Natural law demonstrates its tenuousness by bowing before a greater power.

This was such a time. It was all the more marked because it occurred in a setting of the most tightly structured orderliness. For centuries anything that even threatened to upset the carefully devised routine was considered a desecration. So great was the rigidity now that the meaningful had become meaningless. Order had become the god, and ritual, the sacrament.

To this place, which had become a shrine of human tradition, there came like an explosion of sunlight in the depths of darkness a freeing, unstructured burst of superhuman power.

Of royal colors was the veil. "Blue, and purple, and scarlet, and fine twined linen of cunning work."[1] With the force of a thunderbolt, with unexplained energy from beyond the human spectrum, unseen hands tore it apart. With shock and terror the hitherto complacent priests saw their sacred holy of holies exposed.

God must have wished it otherwise. He would have preferred the hands of men to perform the task, for that is the way He likes to work in this world. He would have desired it a time of joy, not fear. Celebration, not shock. With the crowds gathering round the temple singing hymns of praise, with the city watching, with the world watching, the curtain could have been brought down and neatly folded to accompanying shouts of triumph, with ringing hosannas. But what man will not do God must do. "And Jesus cried with a loud voice, and gave up the ghost. And the veil of the temple was rent in twain from the top to the bottom."[2]

With what eagerness the Father must have been awaiting the opportunity to tear that piece of cloth! It was His first act after the death of His Son. It was accomplished instantly!

While the cross has come to symbolize the events of that great hour, a more enlightened Christendom might have come to ponder with equal solemnity and holy awe the emblem of a torn curtain. With all our steeples and bells and naves and founts, in our stained glass renderings of doves and fish, pomegranates and lilies, where is to be found the symbol of the rent veil?

Some say, "Oh, it was only to mark the end of the old Jewish system." But it means so much more! It is, best of all, a sign of a great beginning—celebration of a new day for humankind. The barrier of sin that had for so long separated men from their Maker had been rolled away by the death of Jesus. Christ had gained for men not forgiveness of sin only, but also *the right of direct access to the very presence of God.*

Divinity's best gift to humanity is *not* eternal life. Salvation means so much more than living forever. Indeed, the perpetuation of life indefinitely could be punishment, not pleasure; hell, not heaven. The great legacy of the cross then is that it offers a *quality* life without end. It has always been that the quality of life exists in direct proportion to the intensity of man's relationship with God. Christ died not only to provide forgiveness of sin, not only to bequeath life eternal, but to restore in our souls the image and character, the very presence and personality of God Himself. This is, after all, the real purpose of our existence. In the Jerusalem temple that momentous day two thousand years ago God *rent* the veil—His way of announcing that every person might have intimate oneness with Him, a oneness capable of restoring men to the likeness of God.

The Old Testament tabernacle was divided into three areas. There was the outer court with its altar and laver. Here sacrifices were performed and the priest could wash himself. The priests ministered daily in the holy place of the sanctuary. It contained the graceful golden candlestick and the table of shewbread, reminders of a day when Someone would come who would be the Light of the world and the Bread of Life.

The third section was most special. It was called the holy of holies. Though the priests went into the holy place each day to sprinkle the blood of the sacrifices there, the high priest alone could enter within the veil into the third compartment of the sanctuary. And even he could enter only once each year—on the Day of Atonement—into that holy of holies where the ark of the covenant was kept. That ark held the Ten Commandments given to Moses by God on Mount Sinai. Upon it was the mercy seat. Here, between the golden wings of the protecting cherubim, shone the very Presence of God Himself. "The glory of the Lord filled the tabernacle,"[3] the Bible says. Sacred, mysterious mixture of fire and light! The Holy Shekinah, without which the sanctuary of Israel would have been merely another building, their form of worship another meaningless ritual not unlike that of their pagan contemporaries.

Yes, at the heart of their worship was the flame of the Presence. God was there always waiting, just within the veil. Today, it must not be forgotten that at the heart of Christianity there is the presence of the heavenly Father. He is the center of it all. God, waiting. Waiting for His modern children to step through the veil, now torn. Miraculously torn, opening the way for all to come straight into the divine Presence.[4]

Tragically, though most Christians may understand their legal right to have access to the throne room of God now, few move into a *personal* experience and consciousness of His presence. The opening of the way to oneness with God is much more than merely a doctrine to be understood or a pardon to be accepted. It is, instead, an entire way of being, an entire way of life to be lived and enjoyed.

Through what Christ has done for us, you and I can live every moment of our lives in the very Presence of Divinity! No longer does the Shekinah glory reflect against the walls of some remote desert sanctuary. God no longer dwells in temples. He dwells in human beings! "In whom ye also are builded together for an habitation of God through the spirit."[5]

Supreme privilege, ultimate opportunity! To be the citadel of God on earth. To give God an expression in flesh and blood in our time. To allow ourselves to be the crucible where divinity and humanity meet and merge. This is the unique prerogative extended to every Christian. Hard-won spoil from the battle of the cross, to ignore this special calling is to blaspheme the blood that makes it possible. "But now in Christ Jesus ye who sometimes were far off are made nigh by the blood of Christ."[6]

The nighness, the nearness, the oneness with God that Jesus' sacrifice has made possible should be reality for every believer. This is Heaven's best gift to mankind. With what radiant wonder should it be contemplated. With what eager expectancy should it be accepted. Bountiful fountain of love, source of unquenchable joy, it is truly the beginning of heaven on earth.

The inhabitancy of God with man today must be regarded with the same reverent awe which early Israel held the Holy Presence in its most sacred place.

Imagine the thrill the timid village girl Mary felt when she began to comprehend the significance of it all! The created to help "create" the Creator! Her God was to be formed within her own body! She had been chosen to give flesh and blood to Divinity!

Today, every believer is called to the kind of awesome responsibility Mary was. Christ was formed physically in her womb. *Now He asks you to allow Him to be formed spiritually in your heart*. "Christ in you, the hope of glory,"[7] promises the Bible. Just as Mary was overcome with awe at the prospect of the Saviour being shaped within her body, with what great reverence should you and I contemplate the promise of Divinity to make our frame and soul Their abode.

Jesus must have resembled Mary in His physical appearance just as any child might reveal some of the characteristics of his mother. Friends might have commented that He had Mary's gentle eyes or her firm chin. She must have been pleased to see her traits in her son. Divinity was encompassed and manifest through form and characteristics contributed by a Jewish maid.

If Christ is permitted to indwell you, your eyes too will come to reflect His peace. Your countenance, the very set of the expression of your face will mirror His benevolent love. The tone of your voice will reveal His patient kindliness. *Your traits can depict God*. Your soul and body can serve as His temple.

Even the greatest artist can do nothing without a canvas on which to work. Your life can become the medium which displays the glory of God.

The torn veil. Miracle. Pronouncement of a new and living way. Passport to the holy of holies. Promise of oneness with Divinity.

2
To Know Him

This is life eternal, that they might know thee the only true God, and Jesus Christ, whom thou hast sent. John 17:3.

I have always felt incomplete because I never knew her. They say she was very fun loving. I can see it in her smile—gentle, promising, yet with a trace of mischievousness. From the pictures, yellowing now, I can tell she was beautiful. A soft glow to her skin. Brown hair cascading down to her shoulders.

Even when I was small I always said I wanted to marry only a brunette. And I did. Whenever I met anyone who had known her I always asked them to tell me everything they could remember about her.

Traveling, riding horses, flying airplanes, she must have been very adventuresome, this pretty girl. She was determined and committed too, or she would not have been involved in an enterprise so daring. She was training to fly bombers to Russia during World War II when she was killed in a tragic accident.

I was only two years old then. Try as I might I have never been able to remember her. My mother formed me, yet I never knew her. There is still a longing that has never been completely filled. The incompleteness I felt especially as a child has never totally disappeared because I missed most of a relationship I was created to have.

Saint Augustine, speaking of man's need for a relationship with God, said, "Thou hast formed us for thyself, and our hearts are restless till they find rest in thee." A loving grandmother helped me compensate for the mother I never knew—but no one can take the place of God in a person's life. Just as a child is born with deep physical and emotional needs that only a mother's love can fill, so everyone is created with an inherent spiritual need. Only knowing God personally can satisfy it.

C. S. Lewis once wrote, "God made us: invented us as a man invents an engine. A car is made to run on petrol, and it would not run properly on anything else. Now God designed the human machine to run on Himself. He Himself is the fuel our spirits were designed to burn, or the food our spirits were designed to feed on. There is no other. . . . God cannot give us a happiness and peace apart from Himself."[1]

Indeed, man is so made that he does not truly live apart from personal, daily, intimate communion with God. He is simply incomplete without it. Many Christians mistakenly assume because they have "accepted" or "found" God at some point in their lives that they are now acquainted with Him. However, there is a vast difference between accepting the Father and knowing Him.

I accept and respect the governor of my state of Alaska as its leader. I even recognize and submit myself to his legal position of authority and power. This does not mean that I know him personally. I cannot claim to know him as a friend.

Sadly, many believers attempt only to benefit from a legal arrangement with God. They proclaim allegiance to His position and authority, but approach no closer. They bring their spiritual life only as far as the outer court of the temple without ever pressing on within the veil to the holy of holies, there to come into the personal presence of the Almighty God.

Christianity today desperately needs the reminder that at its very heart, there must lie a deep, continuous interchange of love and thought flowing directly between the individual believer and God. The Bible writers were men who had a passion for knowing God. We have drifted into such clumsy substitutes for this vital encounter that I wonder whether we can even understand these words of David: "As the hart panteth after the water brooks, so . . . my soul thirsteth for God, for the living God."[2] "My soul followeth hard after thee."[3]

Among our liturgies and litanies, our creeds and cantatas, I am wondering if we have somewhere misplaced the personal reality of our God. Will future church historians write that the capacity to worship, truly worship, disappeared sometime at the end of the twentieth century? Are we living in the post-Christian world? Has our quest to define God intellectually become the entire point of our religion?

But to know about God is not *to know* God. Those who would measure their piety by the soundness of their doctrine and the correctness of their theology should weigh carefully this thought from John Wesley: Orthodoxy, or right opinion, is at best, a very slender part of religion.

The devil in hell knows more about God than the most brilliant theologian. But the humblest saint who in the depths of his heart has communion with the Father truly "knows" Him in the best way of all.

God is still to be found and known from His Word. It is not, however, the mere words—or even the exalted concepts—of Scripture that satisfy the longing of the soul. It is having the kind of intimate friendship with God Himself, of which Scripture testifies, that satisfies. Jesus told the biblical scholars of His day, "You study the scriptures, believing that in them you have eternal life; now these same scriptures testify to me, and yet you refuse to come to me for life!"[4]

God chose the loving intimacy of married sex to illustrate the extent of the oneness which God wishes to enter into with His people. One reason adultery is terribly wrong and divorce so markedly tragic is that they blaspheme and debase the meaning of the symbol God chose to represent the very heart of Christianity, the intimate relationship He desires with the individual Christian.

The Bible describes the church as a "bride adorned for her husband."[5] The Song of Solomon presents Christ as a devoted, loving husband delighting in all the charms of his nubile young wife. She symbolizes the believer. When the Old Testament uses the word *know* or *knew* it often involves the married sexual relationship, as in "Adam knew his wife . . . ; and she bare a son."[6] When the same writers talk of "knowing" God, inherent is at least some of the intimacy. Indeed, when "knowing" God is carried to its fullest extent spiritually, the believer *does* have a new life created within him also. The life of Christ.

All the parallels can perhaps not be appropriately appreciated by a modern generation which has lost much of its purity. Nonetheless contemplation of the theme can lead one to begin to grasp the intensity of the oneness God desires with His people, a oneness reaching far beyond a mental assent to God's authority, the acceptance of a legal pardon from sin, or an intellectual knowledge of His Word.

A. W. Tozer has written: "The Bible is not an end in itself, but a means to bring men to an intimate and satisfying knowledge of God, that they may enter into Him, that they may delight in His Presence, may taste and know the inner sweetness of the very God Himself in the core and center of their hearts."

"The modern scientist has lost God amid the wonders of His world; we Christians are in real danger of losing God amid the wonders of His Word."[7]

There were certain believers while Jesus was on earth who attained a special intimacy with the Master that is a wonderful example for men today. The temperamental John or the former prostitute Mary certainly had no better scriptural or theological training to prepare them for a deeper closeness to Christ than anyone else living then. Yet they were able to enter into a great friendship with Jesus. It is said that John wrote with a pen dipped in love. The deepest insights, the greatest truths Christ taught are revealed most profoundly in his writings.

Jesus did not play favorites, but those who were more openhearted, teachable, and persistent in seeking were able to enjoy a unique, communing fellowship with Him.

Martha busied herself with her pots and pans in the kitchen. Mary knelt eagerly at the feet of Jesus, catching every word, following every expression on His face.

An important spiritual rule is that God does not give something to someone unless he wants it badly enough to take great interest in it, to constantly pursue it, to go outside the routine of ordinary life to find it. More than anything else there is a peristence at *seeking* which is necessary to bring the believer from a nominal adherent to a devoted disciple. It is not dependent on intellectual ability, self-generated piety, or theological training. This persistence at seeking is what makes the difference. That is all. Seeking moves one from a surface religious experience to a deep communion with the living God. It is the tenaciousness of Jacob wrestling with the angel, refusing to let him go until he was blessed. It is the importunity of the man who kept knocking on the door of his neighbor's house until he secured the needed loaves of bread. It is the persistence of the widow who at last won satisfaction from the unjust judge. It is the absolute dedication of the man who sold all that he had in order to buy the field to get the pearl of great price. It is the devotion and discipline of the Master "rising up a great while before day" or going alone at night "up into a mountain apart to pray."[8]

To truly come to know God one must make it the ultimate aim of his life. All other interests, all other activities must be subordinate to it. It must become the ground for one's being, the exciting purpose for one's very existence. There is no higher calling, no greater adventure, no worthier enterprise. This pivot point of life is what gives the rest of living significance. Career or family life do not suffer from giving this quest first priority. They are remarkably enhanced by it. "Seek ye first the kingdom of God, and his righteousness," Jesus said, "and all these things shall be added unto you."[9]

He who has God, has everything. Anyone who knows God is already rich. Material things can never enslave him, for he is not dependent upon them for happiness or satisfaction.

It is sad that some of the *things* God gives have been allowed to take the place of God Himself. To have God's blessings is not necessarily to have God. To enjoy the gift is not necessarily to enjoy the Giver. You can express appreciation to God for some particular thing He has given you. This is giving thanks. You would do the same to the stranger on an airplane who gives you his newspaper to read. On the other hand you acclaim and glorify your heavenly Father for being the sort of God who is generous beyond measure, whose nature is all-forgiving, all-loving. This is praise. This is worship. To give thanks you only have to know about the gift. But to give praise you must know the Giver personally.

Pursuing the kingdom of God is an intense experience. "If . . . thou shalt seek the Lord thy God, thou shalt find him, if thou seek him with all thy heart and with all thy soul."[10] To truly know God is to be assimilated into Him. It is to live every moment as if you were in His presence—because you are! It is to make every thought and action subject to Him. It is to live in an attitude of constant communion with Him.

In the hour of final judgment many will stand before God, claiming to be His people because they have believed He existed and died for them. They may have even accepted His authority and searched His Scriptures and taken His name upon themselves, yet God will have no choice but to pronounce the fateful words to them, "I never knew you."[11]

To know and be known of God is everything. Now and eternally. "And this is life eternal, that they might know thee the only true God."[12] The modern Christian must sweep away from him all the artificial trappings of religion that surround him on every side today so that he can exclaim wholeheartedly with Paul, "O the depth of the riches both of the wisdom and knowledge of God."[13] "I count all things but loss for the excellency of the knowledge of Christ Jesus my Lord."[14]

3
To Be One

That they all may be one; as thou, Father, art in me, and I in thee, that they also may be one in us. John 17:21.

There was once an old Lancashire woman who was listening to a group of her friends discussing the remarkable success of the new minister in their village. Some praised his heart-stirring sermons. Others complimented his friendliness and refined manners. Someone remarked that his proficiency must result from the excellence of his schooling. Someone insisted that his ability to get along well with everyone was a natural gift. "Nay," broke in the old woman, "I will tell you what it is. Your man is very thick with the Almighty!"

A man I do business with told me that he had decided he must be a success. "I can't even think of enough ways to spend all my interest," he said.

Money, position, knowledge, power, talent, psychological insight, sex appeal—by the degree which they possess these, people measure their worth!

After earning his doctorate in theology, a college religion teacher told me he felt successful at last. "It was probably the ultimate accomplishment of my life," he declared.

Piety, chastity, morality, sagacity—by such standards many gauge their spiritual worth. When, I wonder, are we going to begin to judge our success by the single thing that matters most of all? *The ultimate criterion of success is the degree of oneness we enjoy with our God.*

For a sixth-grade correspondence-course assignment my daughter had to make up a series of epitaphs engraved on imaginary tombstones. She had to describe in one sentence the life of each character. While I was helping her with it, my eleven-year-old asked me, "Daddy, what would you like written on your tombstone?" Tough question. If my college professors had posed a few like that, I might have framed my diploma and hung it on the wall instead of filing it away in a cardboard box with my lawn-mower warranty.

Some of the traditional etchings on headstones ran through my mind—"devoted husband, loving father" and "here lies the biggest fool in the cemetery" occurred to me. What would you write about yourself? Perhaps the best that could be written about any one of us would come very close to the words used by the old English woman to describe the pastor: "He was thick with the Almighty." Or maybe "He walked with God." Or "He was one with God."

There is an idea going around that God wants to help people improve their natures. He would really rather not. Instead, He wants to give you a *new* nature. His very own. You are to discard yours and take His.

Christianity does not just save you. "I know that," you say. "It also makes me into a better person."

Sorry, that's wrong! The religion Jesus Christ teaches is revolutionary. It does not round the rough edges off the old personality. It does not design to remodel you into an improved edition of your old self. *It transforms you into an entirely new creature*!

The whole thing is not the little bud blossoming into the gorgeous full-blown flower. It is instead the ugly thistle transforming into a rose! It is the ugly, clinging chrysalis metamorphosing into a radiant, free butterfly.

Psychology speaks of insight. Education speaks of growth, of improvement. Christianity alone can truly speak of transformation. It does not whisper this lightly. It trumpets this personality-shaking, mind-bending revolutionary offer to all. "Therefore if any man be in Christ, he is a new creature."[1] "Be ye transformed by the renewing of your mind, that ye may prove what is that good, and acceptable, and perfect, will of God."[2]

Religion or even psychological knowledge can bring positive change in the existing nature. *Oneness with God transfigures a person with a radically new nature.*

If they were both offered to you free, which would you prefer to have—a brand-new car or a "reconditioned" old one—especially if you realized you were going to travel from here to eternity in it?

Oneness with God is the bench-mark of success, the center point of experiential Christianity, because through it, transfused to humankind, comes the life, the very nature of Christ. Remember from the first chapter that knowing God intimately allows Christ to be conceived within the believer. The communion service—so often celebrated by the believer without awareness of its deeper meanings—helps to reveal in physical terms the reality of His willingness to enter and become one with the believer. Jesus did not set the cross aside as a symbol of His ministry. His followers did that. The Master always intended that the Lord's Supper should remain the high commemorative occasion for reminding us not only of what He did on Calvary, but also of what He does or wants to do for us now.

"Take, eat," He instructed; "this is my *body*." "Drink ye *all* of it," said He, "for this is my *blood*."[3] Christianity is so much more than proper ethics or orthodox religion. It is not just something mental or moral. It is God infusing His people with Himself. It is the believer performing a physical act of worship as he lifts the bread of life to his mouth and takes the "body" of Christ into himself. It is the transfusion of the "blood" coursing throughout his entire system renewing every cell. Do not dare to talk of being "in Christ" in terms of some abstraction, some metaphysical puzzle. Nor speak of Christ being "in you" as some hypothetical state of bliss realizable now only in theory. A definite incoming of divinity into humanity is available right now! It is far more than a misty symbol of a future reality. Far more than a transcendent mental concept. "Ye are the temple of the living God; as God hath said, I will dwell in them, and walk in them; and I will be their God, and they shall be my people."[4]

Christian, your hands are to become the hands of God to work His will in this world. He wants to use your muscles and your cells to be His own! This is what Jesus came to do. He was God on earth in flesh and blood. God can work best with people that way. When humanity and divinity were united in Jesus it started the greatest revolution ever seen. It split time and history in half. It sent the universe reeling. It unseated the unholy prince of this world. God now wills to carry on that revolution through you. You and I indeed have the privilege of bringing it to its climax. Now is the finest hour for Christians. God wants your mind too. "Let this mind be in you, which was also in Christ Jesus."[5] God pours His reasoning powers into the minds given over to Him, and we can think more clearly than ever before. He put His love in us, and we become gentle and kind. Ordinary people become extraordinary people. I hope by now you can see that we are not talking about fanciful theory or spiritual speculation. *Oneness with God is a supra-scientific, supra-biological fact.* The Father's best offer to us is His promise to share immediately in the life and glory and nature of His Son. In our present bodies. In our present minds. We cannot understand this or explain it. But we can experience it.

Only one thing is necessary for this to become a possible reality for the Christian. There must be a setting aside, an extinguishing, of one's own nature. So they can encounter the remarkable transformation urged in Romans 12:2, Paul pleads with all believers to do something first. "I beseech you therefore, brethren, by the mercies of God, that ye present your bodies a living sacrifice, holy, acceptable unto God, which is your reasonable service."[6] In the man-God relationship there remains something for the Christians to *do*—this daily offering up of the self is it!

Jesus shocked people when He said that in order to keep your life you must give it up. The concept of dying in order to live has never been well understood. Certainly it has never been popular. It would not likely push a book to the top of the current self-help reading charts. Today, when the emphasis is on "being your own best friend" and "looking out for number one," most people are tuned into looking inward to self for renewal, inspiration, and purpose.

Christ still insists that fulfillment comes in quite a different way. "Verily, verily, I say unto you, Except a corn of wheat fall into the ground and die, it abideth alone: but if it die, it bringeth forth much fruit. He that loveth his life shall lose it; and he that hateth his life in this world shall keep it unto life eternal."[7] "Whosoever will come after me, let him deny himself, and take up his cross, and follow me. For whosoever will save his life shall lose it; but whosoever shall lose his life for my sake and the gospel's, the same shall save it. For what shall it profit a man, if he shall gain the whole world, and lose his own soul?"[8]

When the true believer wishes to measure his success he does not ask, "How much have I got?" His real question always is, "How much have I given up?" That is the way to genuine prosperity, authentic riches. "Am I giving up enough of self so the nature of Christ is replacing my own?" "Am I beginnng to share in the divinity of the Master?" These are the sort of questions asked in the highest university in the universe.

The best message of the gospel is that the Son of God became a man so that men can now commence to become the sons of God. "But as many as received him to them gave he power to become the sons of God."[9]

After almost 2000 years the full impact of this heavenly offer is still not grasped. Many are afraid to take it for what it really says. Too afraid of the drastic, sweeping changes this may make in their lives. The voice of God is still calling every believer to that high way. To become Jesus Christ by taking His nature into your body and mind. Not merely to become *like* Jesus Christ, but to *become one* with Jesus Christ.

"Now wait just a moment," you say. "That is almost blasphemous." "That is impossible." And it is impossible all right. Impossible like an oak coming from an acorn. Impossible like a butterfly coming from an ugly worm. Impossible as a human being—who grows to be six-foot-four and able to manufacture cornflakes or play Bach on the harpsichord or fly a space shuttle—coming from a single cell invisible to the naked eye.

"This man blasphemeth," the scribes exclaimed

when Jesus dared to tell a young invalid his sins were forgiven. This was the Lord's quick response: "Whether is easier, to say, Thy sins be forgiven thee; or to say, Arise, and walk? But that ye may know that the Son of man hath power on earth to forgive sin, (then saith he to the sick of the palsy,) Arise, take up thy bed, and go unto thine house."[10]

Since the beginning God has always displayed His miraculous power in the physical realm so that men might trust Him when He says He will work miracles for them in the spiritual. Most are so blinded from looking for success in the wrong places they no longer see the real marvels and miracles even in the physical world. *The veil that needs tearing now is that of our own selfish natures.* It must tear if we are going to see into the holy of holies, if we would find oneness with God.

To the priest involved in the ordinary humdrum of daily duties He was just another baby boy, another child to consecrate and for whom to collect the temple fee. If he had been told that in his arms he cradled his Creator, he would surely have said, "Why, that's impossible! He's just flesh and blood like anyone else." But to old Simeon, "just and devout" and filled with the presence of God, that bundle of babyhood was what he had lived to see. It was the miracle he had been waiting for. "For mine eyes have seen thy salvation," he exclaimed with deepest joy. With a vision an entire nation, an entire world lacked, he saw "a light to lighten the Gentiles, and the glory of thy people Israel."[11] Only like can appreciate like. Those who do not discover oneness with God now will be ill-prepared to recognize His Son as their Saviour when He comes again the second time. Because the old man had given his life to becoming one with God he could comprehend and appropriate to himself the Father's great, "impossible" gift to the world. Tragically, today many are like the priest. They cannot see the miracle that God offers us now. It seems impossible that the Father actually offers the very nature of His Son to men and women.

"For with God nothing shall be impossible,"[12] the angel assured Mary when she wondered how Christ could actually be formed inside *her*. When God says He is willing to transfuse the divine nature into the believer, then from the lips of every Christian should come the eager cry, "Let it be!" The trusting peasant girl stated it most beautifully: "And Mary said, Behold the handmaid of the Lord; be it unto me according to thy word."[13]

How the heart of God longs to hear that same response today! The word of promise still comes ringing down. "The glory which thou gavest me I have given them; that they may be one, even as we are one. I in them and thou in me."[14]

Inherent in the word of God for every believer is a nature like Christ's that is from beyond this world. "I have given them thy word; and the world hated them, because *they are not of the world*, even as I am not of the world."[15]

It is not more impossible that God can begin to put the nature of His Son in us than it is that He can save us from sin. Both are miracles. Both are received by surrender and faith. Though they be beyond our human understanding, both are to be simply accepted as they are offered by believers who can say, "Be it unto me according to thy word."

When the young cripple heard the word of Christ to him saying, "Arise, take up thy bed, and go unto thine house," he did not say, "Well, I don't see how I can do that." Nor did he exclaim, "That seems impossible to me!" Instead, he eagerly decided to accept without hesitation what was offered him. He immediately put his will into making an effort to rise. In the willing, *as he began* to act, he was healed. The miracle was wrought.

So you and I may arise like the phoenix from the crippling hold our old, death-destined nature of sin has on us. As we will to accept God's offer we may come to live above immobilizing selfishness. He offers the very nature of His Son. By this means eternal life becomes ours, for Christ has a nature over which death has no power. As we assimilate Him we assimilate eternity!

All in all, the Christian must remember he has one thing to *do* in his spiritual life. Everything else truly is a matter of faith and trust and belief. But there is still one thing he must *do* to be saved and to be transformed. It is to keep on seeking, to keep on placing one's self in the divine presence, to keep on practicing a conscious awareness of God, to keep on willing to be one with Him. For it is from this oneness there comes continuing natural transference of God into His people.

One cold fall day, after spending most of my life watching enviously as many of the birds in the state abandoned Alaska each autumn for warmer places, I decided that they had something to teach me. So I packed my wife and two children into our motor home, and we began to follow the birds' lead. Since I was writing a book I could take my work with me. This gave us an unrestricted schedule. We decided that our only goal should be to follow the sun—not with respect to its daily westward journey, but to its annual southward trek. We traveled until we found warm weather. Then we would camp. After a time the colder weather would catch up with us. The chill in the night air and changing colors of the leaves on the trees would tell us, "Time to move on." And we would be off following the sun.

We journeyed thus through the Yukon Territory. We visited relatives in British Columbia and Washington. Then we moved down the coast of Oregon and through the redwoods to southern California. We laughed merrily when telephoned reports from home told of temperatures of thirty degrees below zero or blizzards producing waist-deep snow.

When the Golden State had a little cold spell we headed for the deserts of Arizona. Eventually our quest led us into Mexico.

To bask in its warmth, you must follow the sun. You must stay as close to it as you can. Likewise, to bask in the warmth of God's love you must follow the Son! Better yet, you must become one with Him. This must become your supreme quest.

C. S. Lewis describes in his unique way how the Christian can partake of the nature of Christ: "If you want to get warm you must stand near the fire: if you want to be wet you must get into the water. If you want joy, power, peace, eternal life, you must get close to, or even into, the thing that has them. They are not a sort of prize which God could, if He chose, just hand out to anyone. They are a great fountain of energy and beauty spurting up at the very centre of reality. If you are close to it, the spray will wet you: if you are not, you will remain dry. Once a man is united to God, how could he not live forever? Once a man is separated from God what can he do but wither and die?"

"Christ is the Son of God. If we share in this kind of life we also shall be sons of God. We shall love the Father as He does and the Holy Ghost will arise in us. . . . Every Christian is to become a little Christ. The whole purpose of becoming a Christian is simply nothing else."[16]

4
To Worship Him

Give unto the Lord the glory due unto his name: bring an offering, and come before him: worship the Lord in the beauty of holiness. 1 Chronicles 16:29.

Once a very devout worshiper prayed at regularly scheduled times each day. Eagerly and aggressively he tried to interest others in the spiritual life he enjoyed. Adoring, pious, reverent, spiritually-minded, fervent, and deeply sincere, he had only one problem with his religious life—*the object of his ardent veneration was the Statue of Liberty.*

Not so much unlike this misguided fellow are some who profess to worship God today. They center their spiritual life around an ideal, not a person. God is regarded as little more than another name for goodness or truth or the principle of love.

The shallowness of our inner spirituality and hollowness of our worship show us how little we know our God.

How sad that the enemy has almost succeeded in causing mankind to lose sight of the personhood of God. Masterful scheme: Bring men to worship a God who is only the *symbol* of the reality. Lead them to regard Him as merely a master computer or a distant energy source. Let Him be considered afar off, a remote, impersonal, incomprehensible mystery. Never, never allow Him to be considered even for a moment as a person, as an approachable, eager friend. How amazingly well the deceiver has succeeded in giving God a bad press.

After all, who would bother to seek out oneness with an idealistic concept? Whose heart would pant after a distant, solemn jurisprudent? Who would care to practice a daily conscious awareness with a mystical life-force?

Tragically, to many religious people God is more of an inference than a reality. "There's just got to be some explanation for the universe," say they, "so to make it make sense, there must be a God." Perhaps they think they are being heroically supportive of Christianity to make such a statement. But merely deducing there is a God from the external evidence that is around—even believing in such a God—is a far cry from *knowing* Him personally. Even the very devils doomed to a hell believe there is a God. To really know and worship God we must come to see Him as a splendid Person. In Christ He is a human person such as you and I. But as God the Father He is a spiritual Person who makes more of a person.

God has a heart that keenly feels. He is capable of every emotion from anger to anguish. He despairs, He wills, He enjoys, He laughs, and He cries. You are in fact capable of making Him cry. You can bring a shadow across the heart of this mighty Being. He exists in a state of infinite sensitivity to not only what you do but also, and even more, to what you are becoming. As you fulfill the purpose for which He created you, and as you begin to respond to Him in worshipful love, you bring the deepest joy to this greatest of Persons.

God experiences every feeling, every delicate emotion, in a momentously more vivid and intense way than we. He is so much a Person that His anguish is deeper, His joy higher and purer than we can possibly imagine. Even a sparrow cannot fall to the ground without the Father's participating sympathy!

Within the depths of that mighty nature, there is enough unique, superhuman individuality to draw you in an eternal quest in knowledge, in oneness, in awareness of Him for time unending. Our highest privilege is to begin immersing ourselves in that amazing, unfathomable Personhood right now. On the tender breast of this living, caring Person every believer may throw himself with complete self-abandon. This is Christianity. This is worship. Worship involves incorporating for one's own self this marvelous divine Being and living to relate deeper and deeper in thought and in love to Him.

There is much talk about believing in a God who should be feared and obeyed. But many have forgotten David's advice: "Delight thyself also in the Lord."[1] Appropriate as the other responses are, this is the one God yearns for most. You can believe in the logic of a Creator-God. You can fear and respect an authority figure, lawgiver, and judge. But you can only delight yourself in a Person, One whom you love deeply.

How very sad that God is often worshiped only for the "becauses." "Because He is all-powerful." Or "because He will judge all someday." Or "because He made us." How much of the love you have for your mother stems from the fact that she produced you biologically? Do you not treasure her most for the kind of person she is to you? Our daughter is adopted, but she loves her mother just as deeply as our son does who is biologically our own. If your father is a judge or a minister or a physician, you might respect his position, wisdom, expertise, professional competence, and intelligence, but this does not increase your love for him one whit. Your affection for your father is seated in the special kind of a person he is to you, in the individual you know him to be, not in the fact that he had something to do with forming you biologically or because he carries some special role or title in society. The edifice of our relationship with God should rest on the foundation of the kind of person He is. It should not rest merely on His power over us or His many splendid attributes or His infinitely superior intellect. The man who shared in my own conception is someone I owe gratitude to for my existence. As another human being whom I only really became acquainted with after I was an adult myself, I respect him and have come to feel a degree of affection for him. But I have never been able to bring myself to feel natural calling him dad or even father. Due to circumstances beyond his control he was not able to be a part of my growing up. The man for whom I feel the very deepest affection as a father is someone else. Yet as this man came into my life as a young boy and as I came to know him as my father-person, the deepest ties developed between us. Our relationship became very close and deep only because we grew to know each other as persons.

God would like us to love Him best just because we have come to know Him as a person. I know few famous people, but one person I am acquainted with in this category is always afraid that people will be attracted to him just because of his status or his wealth. God has real problems with this too. Or perhaps it would be better to say that men have the problem. Many never get beyond the surface attractions to the real divine Being.

People like best to be loved just as they are. Not for

their accomplishments or their riches or their status. While they do not object to being respected for such, they do not want the love others hold for them to be contingent on it. So God does not want us merely to love Him only for the great and good things He is capable of doing for us. Appreciate Him for it, yes. Respect and honor Him for it, yes. But when you really love God, take a lesson from how He loves you. *Love Him best simply for Himself*. When you come to see God as the splendid Person He really is, you cannot help but love Him genuinely. To know this special Person is to love Him.

God is truth, says the Scripture. Certainly, but better than that He is a totally truthful Being. God is love. True, but better yet He is a loving Person. This sort of God can be worshiped with not only the head, but the heart. He is not just a principle but a Person of principle.

As we come to discover God as He really is, not as the enemy has accustomed us to imagine Him, we will be deeply moved and changed. We will come to *want* to diminish our own identity. We will crave more of His nature within us as we immerse ourselves in His divine Personhood. We have only just begun to discover the great joy of worship. It can become a great, lifelong, exciting adventure.

So many cheat themselves and God by thinking that worship is something you only do in church once a week. "The worship hour" we call it, as if when it is over, worshiping is over for seven days. But corporate fellowship, as important as it is, should be only a small slice of the pie of one's devotional life. Indeed, if God is not constantly worshiped in the heart, public worship may have little meaning or value.

How much there is still to learn from Brother Lawrence. The inspiring influence of this seventeeth-century lay brother reaches down into our day. His given name was Nicholas Herman. He came from the Lorraine area of France. He was a simple, unlearned peasant who described himself as "a great awkward fellow who broke everything."[2]

After his conversion he decided he wanted to serve God. He considered becoming a priest but feared he did not possess the intellectual ability. He experienced difficulty grasping the finer points of theology. Consequently in 1649 he entered a monastery as a lay brother assigned to the kitchen washing dishes, pots, pans, and utensils.

Here this humble man made a most startling personal discovery which has inspired countless others ever since. Expecting that the sacrifice of his life to the service of God in such unappealing surroundings would result only in a dreary existence for the rest of his days, he at first thought this would be fit penance for his past sins. Much to his amazement, however, he learned through his own personal pursuit of God that if he maintained a constant awareness of his Lord, deep satisfaction and joy could be his under any circumstance.

"We should establish in ourselves a sense of God's presence by continually conversing with Him," he wrote.[3]

One of his best and most familiar statements shows how an intimacy and oneness with God can turn the most routine duty of daily life into an act of worship. "The time of business does not with me differ from the time of prayer, and in the noise and clatter of my kitchen, while several persons are at the same time calling for different things, I possess God in as great tranquillity as if I were upon my knees at the Blessed Sacrament."[4]

Wherever you are, you too can lift up your heart to God and instantly be in a sanctuary. By choosing to turn your inward gaze upon God you may enter in "through the veil" and worship in the holy of holies, even if you are working at your desk or driving your car or standing over the bathroom sink. Since the Father's face is always toward us, it takes only an instant act of the will, and we may be communing with Him anytime, anywhere. With such immediate access to such an amazing, wonderful Being, the truly incredible thing is that we do not more frequently and heartily take advantage of this remarkable privilege won for us at the cross. *It is not that we are "bad"; it is just that we are cheating ourselves of so very much, if we do not.* Instead of focusing on an awareness of the Father we often allow our minds to just drift along, playing back beer or hamburger commercials. At other times our mental powers are captivated by our sexual fantasies or are engrossed with plans for our own self-aggrandizement. Be honest. What do you really think about when you are driving your car, taking a walk, or jogging? Why not devote at least some of your daily, hour-by-hour thought processes to reaching out in communion to God?

Prayer, Bible study, and church attendance are considered the traditional methods of focusing the attention on God. While all these facets of spirituality are extremely important, a person can engage in every one of them consistently and yet be doing them in form only, still missing out on the true practice of the presence of God. What we are attempting to grasp here is a very personal kind of heart-to-heart communion with the Father that reaches new dimensions far beyond even the ordinary concept of prayer and worship. What this generation needs as it stands at the climax of earth's history is a depth of relationship with God never before experienced by a group of Christians. The lives of believers all over the world need to light up brilliantly with the radiance that comes from communing in the holy of holies as the darkness of evil threatens to extinguish all that is good. After Moses had held face-to-face and heart-to-heart communion with God on the mountain, he came down with his face shining. He came down into the camp that was engrossed in evil, yet with God's glory he met the evil and conquered it. "Show me thy glory," he had asked God, and that God did—throughout the rest of his life.

You and I must dare to ask God to show us His glory. We will never be the same, for we will become reflectors of His glory. How badly we need to understand better than we do what the Bible means when it recommends to "do all to the glory of God."[5] *Everything* the believer does can be an act of worship. Even the humblest duties can be performed for God's sake.

If the simplest and most routine thing is done to the honor and glory of God it is then endued with great purpose and satisfaction. This becomes the path to the deepest self-identification and self-worth for the individual. It invests all of life with meaning and wonder. How greatly this is needed at these times when the worth of everything, including life itself, is being questioned in the hearts of so many.

One of the most remarkable things about children—to the envy of adults—is their sense of wonder over even the simplest things. When Jesus said, "Except ye be converted, and become as little children, ye shall not enter into the kingdom of heaven,"[6] I am convinced He was revealing how God prizes people who have not lost their sense of wonder. Those who will enter heaven have been able to take great delight here and now in the greatest source of all wonder, the Lord God. Through the meaning this wonder has infused into their lives, they will be able to capture the significance of every action, every thought, every moment as being vitally important. Important because a close, personal friendship with God makes it so. If you seek meaning in your marriage, meaning in your relationships with your children, meaning in your work, meaning in your Scripture reading, meaning in your prayers, meaning in your church worship, you will find it only in a close, personal, internal friendship with the heavenly Father. Every person must for himself discover his own most effective path to an inner oneness with God. It is not "natural" for any human being to practice the presence of God. We instead tend to center inwardly on ourselves. "We have turned every one to his own way."[7] Only by the most diligent effort of the will may we direct the center focus of our lives away from ourselves and toward God. God must reside at the nucleus of our lives.

Both the *way* and the *degree* that each person accomplishes this focusing will be different. What may draw me in intimacy and awe to God may bring no such response from your heart. On the other hand, what inspires and uplifts you spiritually may provide little meaning to me. We must make allowances for each other in such matters as personal preferences in Christian music, preaching, study, reading, and witnessing. We must be very adventuresome in the way we worship. We must be personally inventive in how we come to practice oneness with God.

The one who has habitually given very little thought to God each day may be making great progress when he reaches the point where he is reflecting on the Father two or three times a day. On the other hand, one who has habitually communed with God morning, noon, and night may find a wonderful growth experience in contemplating the Father for a portion of each hour of the day.

The battle is "dying to self," forming the habit of practicing the presence of God. Today we are bombarded by a greater amount of external stimuli than any other generation in history. Times are more complex. God understands this situation with His infinite sympathy and patience. Do not become discouraged if at first you fail in developing your focus on God. Brother Lawrence said, "I am come to state wherein it would be as difficult for me not to think of God as it was at first to accustom myself to it." Yet this same man also said this: "He lays no great burden upon us: a little remembrance of Him from time to time; a little adoration; sometimes to pray for His grace, sometimes to offer Him your sorrows, and sometimes to return Him thanks for the benefits He has given you, and still gives you in the midst of your troubles. He asks you to console yourself with Him the oftenest you can. Lift up your heart to Him even at your meals and when you are in company; the least little remembrance will always be acceptable to Him."[8]

As you struggle to practice the presence of God, you will come to the end of a day and realize with despair that you have not thought of Him even once. Do not be discouraged. The very fact that you feel bad about such a thing is evidence of your progress. Little by little as the days, weeks, and months go by, communing with Him will become more and more natural for you. The way you do it and the degree you do it will be different from those of other believers, but you will be moving constantly toward the same sacred goal—continual communion with Him. For some this may not be attained fully until heaven. But a great foretaste of the world to come is available to all who now continue to pursue Him to the best of their ability. By disciplining our minds to keep Him in the center focus of our consciousness, you and I may begin to live in a constant attitude of worship. Certainly other activities will go on and other thoughts will at times have to intervene. But the awareness of God may carry over into all these other interests and enterprises. The Father does not leave us out unless *we* leave *Him* out. Everything can be done to His glory. Everything can be an act of worship. The personal presence of God can become what the Father has always intended it to be for us—the central fact, the glory and wonder of our lives.

5
To Be Blessed

Thou wilt keep him in perfect peace, whose mind is stayed on thee. Isaiah 26:3.

In perfectly calm waters I went to sleep down in the cabin. It was our first day at sea, towing a barge loaded with supplies to build a new mission station at a remote Alaskan Eskimo village. I was only a small boy then, but I can still remember snuggling down into the covers in the warm bunk as the gentle motion of the tugboat lulled me to sleep.

In a few hours after we had rounded a cape and were out in the main body of the Bering Sea, a storm came up. With nothing but wind and water between us and the Siberian coastline several hundred miles to the west, large waves had built up quickly. Their thunderous smashing into the plank hull beside my head awakened me. I was terrified. It was dark down in the cabin. I was all alone. The boat seemed to be pitching and bucking terribly. Occasionally an especially large wave would hit like a sledgehammer. The tug would shudder from bow to stern, the wood creaking and groaning in protest. I could hear these big waves wash completely over the deck above my head.

My terror grew when salty water started leaking in

around the hatch, dripping on my bed. It did not take much of that to inspire me to abandon my formerly snug nest. Without bothering with my pants I scrambled frantically through the narrow cabin passageway and clambered up the stairs to the top deck. I was convinced we were headed for the bottom. Trembling, I clutched at my father's pant leg to steady myself as he stood at the wheel.

I was amazed when I looked up at his face. He was smiling! Without looking down at me he said, "I love a brisk wind on the sea like this." I could see that he was actually enjoying guiding the boat through the storm. As I stood close beside him there in the pilothouse, his confidence chased away my apprehension. I, too, soon began to delight in the experience the elements were handing us.

I have never forgotten how my fear disappeared when I came to where my father was.

Someone has written, "The measure of your anxiety is the measure of your distance from God."[1]

Immense, immeasurable, and immediate supernatural blessings spontaneously flow to the believer who makes closeness to and oneness with God his first priority. A sense of abiding peace is only one of these, but it is surely one of the best.

Such peace is possible because closeness to God also brings His protecting presence to surround and cover the life as nothing else can.

"Stay close to me, or I cannot be responsible for your protection," the guard told those of us once who were part of a group visiting a large California prison.

God has repeatedly told us the same thing. He can not preserve and protect from evil those who choose not to walk near Him. And we need protection because this entire world is a gigantic correctional institution.

It is even more like a battle zone. Evil (much of it subtle and unseen), injury, accident, and untimely death are enemies that constantly threaten the lives, well-being, and peace of mind of every person. Tragedy stalks all. Pretending that evil and death do not threaten us does not make them go away.

Think about how you felt the last time your husband or wife or child was unexpectedly several hours overdue coming home from work or shopping or school. We have all experienced it. As the night gets darker, you feel the rising tension, the tightening of the chest, the pounding pulse, the straining of the ears to hear the familiar step at the door.

We well know what at any instant can happen to ourselves or to those close to us. In this imperfect world, one cannot afford to live without a Protector. As time goes on and instability of every kind increases, as economic insecurity spreads like a plague and men begin to admit there are problems the best of their wisdom cannot solve, it becomes more and more obvious that there is no earthly form of security.

What a pity that even so few Christians recognize in practice that God has plainly committed Himself to being completely responsible for those who walk close to Him. When they do this He becomes accountable for their spiritual, mental, and physical safety. The greater the intimacy one experiences with God, the greater the peace and protection a person has. *There is safety in oneness*. "He that dwelleth in the secret place of the most High shall abide under the shadow of the Almighty."[2]

God does not arbitrarily refuse to protect those who do not practice His presence, but He does experience difficulty communicating with them. They do not allow Him to guide and protect them because they are not in the habit of responding to Him. When they are in danger He is not a resource they can draw on, for the channel of communication has not been kept clear. If one allows it the still small voice of guidance or conscience or inspiration that can lead one away from danger and trouble and evil can easily be overridden or drowned out entirely by the raucous clamor of life.

A small plane, flying in the clouds on instruments was repeatedly warned away from a high mountain peak by an air-traffic controller. It crashed into the rocks with the loss of all on board without the pilot's ever making any response to the messages being transmitted so desperately to him. In the wreckage investigators found the volume control on the communications radio turned way down and the volume control on a broadcast band radio tuned to a popular music station turned up high!

While closeness to God is not always a guarantee of physical safety, the point of the Bible teaching on the subject is that *normally* it is. Under unusual circumstances there may be times when God in His providence permits something to happen to one who is near to Him that some would consider a tragedy. Could we see the end from the beginning as God can, we would then define it differently. The assurance is given repeatedly that God will allow only what is for the best good to happen to those who are close to Him. You cannot ask for anything better.

Many feel they cannot trust in God's protection when they see apparently moral, ethical people or even fellow believers experience apparent tragedy. A former classmate of mine recently told me that he had believed in God's special protection over him since childhood. Then a man he admired very much died in a car crash. "Why he was even a minister," my friend said. "If God couldn't protect him, when he was doing so much good, I don't think I could believe He would ever protect me."

The way God chooses to deal with some other person should not prevent your relationship with Him. When Christ gave Peter a remarkable revelation regarding his ultimate fate, Peter should have rested content. Instead, catching sight of the disciple John nearby, he asked compulsively about God's plans for this man. Jesus' quick rebuke was for all spiritual speculators. "Jesus saith unto him, If I will that he tarry till I come, what is that to thee? follow thou me."[3]

Follow thou Me, stay close to Me, Peter. Devote your attention to oneness and trust and love; let those things be your concern, Christ was saying. Then your life can be the simple outworking of God's will and whatever He intends it to be for you.

You and I, like Peter, need to concentrate more on staying close to God, not on questioning God's dealing with some other. If we do this, our safety and salvation and all else will become God's responsibility. He is willing and eager to intervene miraculously time after time in every life that is constantly entrusted to Him.

But don't assume that good behavior or correct religious belief will bring some sort of guarantee of divine protection. These do not bring protection any more than they assure any other blessing from God, such as peace or love or eternal life. Certainly salvation does not come from good behavior. It is given to those who love God and seek oneness with Him in this life. The same is true of protection. If you and I were protected to the degree that we obey God we would all have been overcome long ago!

David provides a good example. The darker side of his conduct ran the gamut from subtle deceit to purposeful adultery and planned murder. Yet the Bible says, "The Lord preserved David whithersoever he went."[4] If God's resources were ever taxed to protect anyone it was certainly this man whose sheep were stalked by lions and charged by bears. A giant more than twice his size and strength was determined to make scavenger food out of him. He was trailed for months by a band of assassins. His king and employer tried to run a javelin through him in close quarters. Even his own son plotted his death. But through everything, in spite of his sins and mistakes, God miraculously preserved and protected him.

Why? Obviously not because of his sin-free life.

God could provide so remarkably for David because, most of all, this Israelite was a man whose habit it was to make first priority in his life the practice of the presence of God. This was what he lived for, his quest: "My heart . . . crieth out for the living God."[5] "Oh that men would praise the Lord."[6] "As the hart panteth after the water brooks, so panteth my soul after thee, O God."[7] He wrote some of the greatest literature in the history of the world, and it was all inspired by his passion to experience intimate oneness with God. His words come ringing down through the centuries, touch other men, and draw them to experience the living God in the center of their souls. "For thou, Lord, hast not forsaken them that seek thee."[8] In this he spoke of himself, for God never forsook him. Not even when he sinned! In fact, it was this same closeness that David achieved with his heavenly Father that could bring him agonizing to his knees in repentance when he did do wrong.

God paid this man the ultimate compliment ever given a human being. "I have found David the son of Jesse, *a man after mine own heart*."[9]

The search goes on. God walks the earth today, still seeking men who will crave His personal presence so much they will be drawn close enough to Him to become men after His own heart.

When He finds someone like this, or rather, when they find Him, nothing is too good for them. You say, "David was especially blessed because he was king." But are we not all now kings—*and* priests? God has so much to give! He is aching to give it, anxious to pour out His blessings, His riches, on a world dying for the want of them. His best gifts He gives through people. Tragically, most never come close enough to Him to benefit themselves or others.

Some Christians are so busy concentrating on themselves or their sins that they have no time for their Saviour. After all, the chief reason selfishness or sin is evil is not the undesirable social effects it produces. It is despicable and destructive primarily because it quickly separates a person from oneness with God. It destroys the very fountain of all life and blessing.

At times God has winked at men's weakness, the Bible says. He understands it. He can overlook our failures and instantly forgive our most heinous mistakes if we sincerely repent and realize with horror how they choke off so quickly our lifeline relationship with the Father. Remember, before the high priest in the Old Testament could go into the holy of holies he had to cleanse and purify himself both physically and spiritually. Most important, he had to have an attitude of openness and reverence toward God. While it is vital to grasp the sinfulness of sin, we must realize that what a man *does* is not quite so important as what he *is becoming* in creative closeness with the Father. This is what most keenly interests Him.

Not perfect belief or even perfect behavior but perfect *intention*. This God values most in every believer. To become a "man after God's own heart," to be truly blessed of God, *the intention, the will, must be profoundly devoted to seeking intimate closeness to the Father.* Nothing is more important spiritually. In a relationship with God, *everything depends on the right action of the will.* Mistakes will still be made, behavior may still fall short of perfection, and faults will create waves on the sea of life. But if the set of the will is solidly secured toward seeking daily, intimate oneness with God, the winds of the Spirit will be caught, and the believer will be propelled into the kingdom of God.

There was another man not without fault either, yet who was paid a terrific compliment by God. He simply and beautifully called him His friend. When this man devoted himself heartily to the pursuit and service of God, the Father poured out such blessings on him their tremendous impact is still warming the world today. "In thy seed shall all the nations of the earth be blessed,"[10] Abraham was told. And they were. And they are still.

"He that abideth in me, and I in Him," said Jesus, "the same bringeth forth much fruit."[11] There is no limit to the good that can come to and through the life of any single person who, putting self aside, will make constant awareness of God the center of his life. This awareness is the ultimate source of good in the world. It is the pipeline of blessings from the kingdom of God in heaven to the kingdom of God on earth.

Once Abraham established closeness with God, nothing was withheld from him. He was protected and prospered in countless ways. "And Abraham was very rich in cattle, in silver, and in gold."[12]

Any person who practices oneness with God will become more prosperous in everything he does. His insights will be greater, his wisdom expanded, his business sense keener. God explicitly wills that every follower should do well in every field of enterprise in which he engages—"Whatsoever he doeth shall prosper."[13] This divine commitment is not made lightly. Nor is it made to apply primarily to material and financial rewards, though by no means does it exclude these things. God never placed a halo around poverty. The God of an abundant creation wants abundance for you—"good measure, pressed down, and shaken together, and running over."[14] Perhaps no nation of the world can actually be called Christian. Nonetheless, do you suppose that it is merely a happy accident that those countries which could most closely fit that description are the most blessed with peace and properity? Think about that.

God's greatest gifts, however, do not come in dollars and can not be measured by the gross national product. They are spiritual.

"When the Lord divided Canaan among the tribes of Israel, Levi received no share of the land," A. W. Tozer once wrote. "God said to him simply, 'I am thy part and thine inheritance,' and by those words made him richer than all his brethren, richer than all the kings and rajas who have ever lived in the world. And there is a spiritual principle here, a principle still valid for every priest of the Most High God.

"The man who has God for his treasure has all things in One. Many ordinary treasures may be denied him, or if he is allowed to have them, the enjoyment of them will be so tempered that they will never be necessary to his happiness. Or if he must see them go, one after one, he will scarcely feel a sense of loss, for having the Source of all things he has in One all satisfaction, all pleasure, all delight. Whatever he may lose he has actually lost nothing, for he now has it all in One, and he has it purely, legitimately and forever."[15]

In spite of his gold, Abraham was never so rich as when God told this man "I am thy shield, and thy exceeding great reward."[16]

The believer who seeks oneness with the Father will soon understand that nothing he has belongs to him anyway. He will come to see himself as he really is—a steward or manager for his Master. A friend of God may have practically everything, but in his heart he will know that he possesses nothing. Or, possessing nothing, yet he may know with a surety that he has indeed everything. The man who is close to God will see the cobwebs of his selfishness and materialism wiped away by the precious, unearthly insights that come from having God in his heart. He will understand that his real treasures are inward and eternal. In a world of accumulators he will know that it is not what one has but what one *is* that is important. While others want to be applauded as "go-getters," he wishes to become a "go-giver." He knows that all good and great things of God must be given away in order to be kept. They must be shared in order to be experienced. When a person receives this unique insight on life through the vision that oneness with God alone can bring, the Father's highest purpose for that individual has been realized. He now has someone who is safe to save and to bless. He can pour out on that individual His best blessings, be they material or spiritual. He knows He is not dumping them in a holding pond to be stored but into a living channel to be distributed to meet the needs of the world.

To Abraham and his children—conditional on their faith—God made some amazing commitments. "The Lord thy God shall bless thee in all thou doest."[17]

"Blessed shalt thou be in the city, and blessed shalt thou be in the field. . . . Blessed shalt thou be when thou comest in, and blessed shalt thou be when thou goest out. . . . And the Lord shall make thee plenteous in goods, in the fruit of thy body, and in the fruit of thy cattle, and in the fruit of thy ground. . . . The Lord shall open unto thee his good treasure."[18]

The good news of Christianity is that the Father intends every believer to be His special friend, just as Abraham was, and to receive His special blessings, just as Abraham did. These blessings are generated by the tremendous new intimacy between God and people that Jesus Christ has won for us. Remember the torn veil? Remember God's invitation to you to join Him personally in the holy of holies? Remember that Christ won for you the right to join Him in the throne room of the universe as a priest and a king? Best of all, hear the joyful proclamation come ringing down from the courts above. "I call you not servants; . . . but I have called you friends."[19] Everything God gave the great spiritual men of the past He is anxious to give to those who seek to know Him intimately today. "That the blessing of Abraham might come on the Gentiles through Jesus Christ."[20] "And if ye be Christ's, then are ye Abraham's seed, and heirs according to the promise."[21]

God wished to bless Abraham and his descendants so that the whole world could see the marvelous benefits of practicing oneness with God. Today, the Father still seeks to attract men to Him by the drawing power of the blessed lives, the remarkable and extraordinary lives, of those who are closest to Him. The day of the chosen people is not over. The waiting world needs to see that oneness with God does indeed produce better people. Quieter, happier, healthier, more radiant people. People who begin where others leave off. People who have something in them that is beyond themselves. Ordinary people—yet pulsating with extraordinary joy and freedom and wisdom and love.

You are called to be that sort of person—God's shining mirror, reflecting the light and blessing of paradise into the shadows of this dark planet. If you want to share the good and great things of God, seek first intimacy with the Father. God's blessings will come to you as the natural result of immersing yourself in Him daily. "Delight thyself also in the Lord; and he shall give thee the desires of thine heart."[22] "If ye *abide* in me, . . . ye shall ask what ye will, and it shall be done unto you."[23]

Begin in your life this process of divinification. Possess the very nature of God forming inside your own self. Know Him more and more as your heart opens more and more to receive His attributes. Know His love and power. Receive the unsearchable riches of Christ. Comprehend more and more "what is the breadth, and length, and depth, and height; and to know the love of Christ, which passeth knowledge, that ye might be filled with all the fulness of God."[24] This is the certain and splendid heritage of every person who makes oneness with the Father his daily quest. To inherit it is to be blessed above all men.

6
To Experience Heaven Now

Jesus came . . . preaching . . . and saying, The time is fulfilled, and the kingdom of God is at hand. Mark 1:14, 15.

Only by diligent inquiry I found it. Seemingly as appreciative of privacy in death as he was in life, Charles Lindbergh chose one of the most remote and lovely sites on earth as his final resting place. At the sparsely settled south end of Maui, accessible only by a narrow country lane, in a setting of utmost serenity and beauty overlooking the shining sea, his remains rest in a tiny graveyard high on a cliff—close to a small, century-old church built by some of the first missionaries to the Pacific.

Large trees, their leaves rustling from the soft ocean breezes, stand as sentinels in the churchyard. A few vividly colored tropical flowers add their comely reds and pinks to the penetrating blue of the sea and sky and the dark green of the dense, tropical foliage. But the poignant inscription on the modest gravestone most impressed me. It caught the spirit of the man whose courage and lone daring gripped the world. It also revealed his personal and less-well-known commitment to a God whom he considered his constant companion on dangerous flights over the most remote sections of the globe anyone had ever ventured to before. It read simply, "If I take the wings of the morning, and dwell in the uttermost parts of the sea."

These words were taken from Psalm 139, which says more fully, "Whither shall I go from thy spirit? or whither shall I flee from thy presence? If I ascend up into heaven, thou art there: if I make my bed in hell, behold, thou art there. If I take the wings of the morning, and dwell in the uttermost parts of the sea; even there shall thy hand lead me, and thy right hand shall hold me."[1]

What a joy to serve a God who is everywhere present, who accompanies us on all our journeys, who promises to remain beside us every step of life's way, who does not forget even our final resting place. Oh, the release and comfort to be found in practicing the presence of, in constantly communing with, this living, loving, always-present God. The Bible says, "In thy presence is fulness of joy; at thy right hand there are pleasures for evermore."[2]

The fact that God is everywhere and openly accessible to men means one startling thing to the Christian—*for the believer heaven begins now*.

While paradise is many-splendored, it is not the streets of gold or the crystal sea that make it heaven. It is instead the intensity of the Person and presence of God which cause it to be utopia for man. Adam dwelt in a perfect heaven on earth. But in this perfect paradise he fell! He fell because he let himself become separated from the presence of God. Lucifer, the archangel, light bearer to the universe, walked the courts of the perfect city of God in the heaven of heavens. But he fell! With direct access to the throne of God he let go his conscious awareness and oneness with the Father.

He put himself on the throne of his own life instead, and created the beginnings of hell in heaven. But Lot continued righteous in Sodom! Christ Jesus kept His purity in the ghetto of Nazareth! Daniel never lost communion with God in the courts of the pagan king. *Heaven is where you make it by the personal communion you chose to have with God!* Heaven is now and always will be a ceaseless approaching to God through Christ. In this continual coming to the Father we begin to receive life eternal and begin heaven here.

A very old catechism asked the question, "What is the chief end of man?" The answer was given: "Man's chief end is to glorify God and enjoy Him forever." As you and I begin to do this, we truly enter into paradise now. That is not to say that there is not a better and more glorious world to come. It is, however, an *extension* of the kingdom of God that is already available to believers who become intimate with the Father. Through this close relationship it is possible to enter into the very atmosphere of heaven on this earth. For those who experience this closeness with God, when their lives end or when Christ comes again, it will then be but a natural transition to move physically into the literal kingdom of heaven. It will be seen as simply another natural step in the sequence of a constantly deepening relationship with the Lord.

As Lucifer and Adam learned so tragically, God is the very fountain of life. Life and heaven can be ours only as we remain in communion with Him. Separated from God, existence may be ours for a little time, but we do not possess eternal life, do not enter into the kingdom of heaven.

Someone once asked Mark Twain the question "Who do you think will get to heaven?" Replied the humorist with a sly smile, "Well, I reckon the folks that get to heaven will be the ones who will feel at home when they arrive." His theology might not have been quite complete, but his point was a good one. Certainly it is only by coming to know God as a friend now, by practicing His presence, by being aware of Him everywhere we go and in everything we do that we prepare ourselves for an eternity of fellowship with Him. "And this is life eternal, that they might know thee the only true God, and Jesus Christ, whom thou hast sent."[3]

The last chapter pointed out how the Father has innumerable blessings He is eagerly waiting to bestow on everyone who draws near to Him. These dynamic qualities and divine treasures sent to earth can bring the very atmosphere of the courts above to this place for you right now. These are such an intrinsic part of the character and riches of God that for those who possess them heaven has indeed begun. Heavenly peace, heavenly love, heavenly joy, heavenly wisdom are only a few of the benefits that come spontaneously into the dedicated life.

I was traveling thousands of miles from home in a foreign country. Other than one or two of the businessmen I had made sales to, no one seemed to speak English. I was beginning to feel quite alone and alienated. In one section of a large city I had gotten lost while trying to find an office where I had an appointment. I tried to use a phone to call a taxi but (1) my coins would not fit in the slots, and (2) when I got the right change the radio dispatcher could not undersand my directions. Giving up on that idea, I started walking in what I hoped was the general direction I was supposed to go, hoping to stumble across the right street sign that would eventually lead me to my destination. I was uneasy doing this, for I had been told robberies of foreigners were not at all uncommon. As I rounded a corner I was overjoyed to sight a red, white, and blue flag flying from a building just ahead. On the front in brass letters were the words "American Embassy." I hurried through the big doors and was immediately greeted by the cheerful voice of a blond receptionist who asked *in English* "May I help you?" From the background came music like that I played at home on my own stereo. Someone was talking in an office with a Texas drawl. Copies of familiar magazines in the reading rack caught my eye. Instantly I felt very much at home. I realized for the first time that, thanks to the embassy system, there are little bits of America scattered all over the world.

God wants little bits of His kingdom scattered all over this planet too. He wants places where the lost can seek help and sanctuary. He wants places on this earth where the atmosphere is like the atmosphere of heaven, where the language spoken is not the harsh speech common to earth but the gentle language of love, kindness, and sympathy.

The Father desires the lives and homes of Christians to be His embassies where His kingdom can be established right now. "Now then we are ambassadors for Christ."[4]

Our local newspaper carried the announcement recently that the President of the United States had chosen a young businessman and politician from our city to be his ambassador to one of the largest South American countries. Friends of mine that knew him commented not only on how hard-working he was but also on how closely his political ideals matched those of the President.

To represent the kingdom of heaven on earth, believers must be very close to the mind of God. Their aim is to reflect the very character, personality, and nature of the Father as perfectly as they can. They must identify intimately with God to do this. His thoughts must become their thoughts, His words their words. In the embassy I visited, the President's picture was displayed prominently on the lobby wall. It was a reminder that what went on there was to be an extension of his will and principles.

Men who choose to accept this role of ambassador must give up their own interests and be willing to represent those of their government.

The forces of spiritual evil fear nothing quite so much as those whose lives are drawn so close into oneness with God that they begin to become a reflection of His character, His will, His principles. Satanic agencies would like nothing better than to stamp out every trace of the kingdom of God from this planet. It is the ultimate challenge today to stand faithfully as a representative of heaven in a dark and dying world. God calls every believer to verify the reality of His kingdom by drawing so near to Him in intimate identification that the atmosphere of heaven will manifest itself on earth through that person. That is how the commonwealth of God is established in this present world. "Thy kingdom come. Thy will be done in earth, as it is in heaven"—and the kingdom is come, not with chariots of fire or clouds of angels just yet, but in the lives of men. It is come in the gentle touch, the sympathetic word, the forgiving smile. If you look for it, you can see it in people—quieter, happier, more radiant people. People who always seem to have a lot of time to do things for others. Men and women who live for persons, not things, who are more concerned with giving than getting. Thus you may find the kingdom—not in earthquake or fire or whirlwind but, strangely enough, just as Elijah found God in the mountain—in the still, small, gentle voices, in open hearts and outstretched hands.

"How foolish the Jews were in Christ's time," we say today. "They expected Him to come and set up a grand, political, rich, material kingdom that would rid them of the Romans and make Jerusalem the center of the world." "They had the very Creator of the universe walking their streets, and they ignored Him." "They could have sat at the feet of the Lord of heaven and listened to His teachings and learned to know Him as Master and Friend, but they were too busy looking for a Messiah-King."

But many Christians today are just as guilty of ignoring their Saviour as were the Jews of old. Some are busy proclaiming that Christ is coming again, focusing exclusively on the glories and beauties of the eternal kingdom to come—the streets of gold, the crystal streams, the fabulous mansions, the gates of pearl—all the wonderful prospects for a joyful reality someday in the future. As worthy and pleasing as these things are to contemplate with anticipation, they do not constitute—nor have ever constituted—the essence of the kingdom of God.

The Jews looked forward to a Messiah who would liberate them from the bondage of Rome sometime in the future, while One walked in their midst at that moment who could deliver them from an inner bondage far more terrible than that enforced by any caesar. "If the Son therefore shall make you free, ye shall be free indeed."[5]

Today there are many who would wait for the glorious coming of the kingdom of God in the future to free them from the sinful habits, the sinful propensities, the sinful attitudes that make life anything but heaven on earth now. But with their focus on the future they may be ignoring the very present Saviour who promises victory over sin in the present tense to those who will abide closely in Him, relying on His Spirit, His power, His presence, to begin eliminating it from their natures *now*.

Not only to the Jews of long ago but also to those today who have lost their spiritual perspective, the voice of Jesus still comes ringing: "For behold, the kingdom of God is within you."[6] And within us it is, a living reality for those who daily walk in close fellowship with God. The supernatural love, peace, joy, and Christlikeness that this available, attainable union spontaneously and miraculously produced is the stuff of eternity to come.

A little girl's father had told her he was going to take her on the best vacation trip ever. The family planned it for weeks. The child could hardly wait for the day to come to leave. As the date approached she kept asking her parents if tomorrow would be the day they would go. Always the answer would be, "Not yet, but it won't be long." The little one could hardly stand the anticipation and excitement. The night before they were actually going to leave, she could scarcely sleep at all. When she awoke the next morning she heard her parents getting things ready to go. She bounded out of bed and ran to her father's arms. "Daddy! Daddy!" she shouted, "*Is this the right tomorrow?*"

The good news for each Christian is that for him *now* can be the breaking of the day that broke at Calvary, *now* the day the curtain tore. This *is* the right tomorrow. Believers need not live in the future, as glorious as it will be, for heaven begins now for everyone who moves into intimacy with God, the God "who hath delivered us from the power of darkness, and hath translated us into the kingdom of his dear Son."[7]

7
To Know the Limits of Reason

Let no man deceive himself. If any man among you seemeth to be wise in this world, let him become a fool, that he may be wise. For the wisdom of this world is foolishness with God. 1 Corinthians 3:18, 19.

Seven-thirty in the morning just has to be the best part of the day in Hawaii. The sun is up high enough to begin clearing the palm trees. The air is fresh and gentle as it flows across the awakening land from the cool, blue sea.

Such splendors greeted me recently as I set out for a morning run along a beach trail on the north shore of Oahu. The sandy path meandered along the surging surf line, rising over coral outcroppings and black lava ledges, then veering inland among lush green shrubbery.

It was here in a quiet clearing just beginning to catch the first, bright rays of the sun, that I saw it.

Now, botanical knowledge have I none. My interest in growing things has usually been limited to a certain vague awareness of their existence and an occasional sense of gratitude that some of them can be eaten and show up on my plate from time to time.

This particular morning, however, I was stopped

short in my tracks by the sight of a lovely, delicate pink flower growing on a bush in that clearing. It faced the rising sun, which was beginning to shine into its open face as if to greet it with benevolence. As I watched in awe, the sun began to light the deep purple center of the flower, which curved daintily down its slender throat. I was enthralled by this object of beauty. I moved close to the flower and put my face close to it. I was filled with joy at its symmetry and loveliness.

Now I did not even know the common name of that flower, let alone the proper scientific designation of its genus and species. I didn't know whether it had sprung from a seed or a bulb or something else. I cannot tell you if it was a perennial or a biennial. This one thing I do know—that morning on the Hawaiian beach I was made a bit more alive, was warmed and charmed by the graceful fairness of that single, comely flower.

For a moment I was tempted to reach out and pick it. I even thought of pulling its silken petals apart to attempt to understand something of the source of its mysterious beauty. But I did not, for I sensed that if I took this dainty, living thing apart, I could never hope to put it back together again. It would have destroyed it, and with it the best of what it meant to me. Far better, I decided, to leave it alone, so that I and others could continue to look at it just as it was and to be touched always by its loveliness.

Returning from my run that day, I took a shortcut across a golf course. There, in the middle of the fairway, was a big, ugly contraption. As I got closer I could see that it was a grass mower, the kind you ride on. It was very ungainly and unappealing to look at, though it obviously served a useful purpose.

I realized as I looked at this monument to man's mechanical cleverness that with the proper tools I could take the mower apart and find out what made it work. Furthermore, I could, with the help of a mechanic with a manual, put it back together, even perhaps improving the function of it a bit as I did so.

To me, Christianity is like the flower, theology like the grassmower. One stands for love and faith, the other for the intellect and reason. Some people get the two mixed up.

To be certain, theology and reason serve a useful purpose for the Christian. The intellectual comprehension of one's religion is both necessary and important in the proper context. It is just that it is most distressing to see miscellaneous, greasy bits of mechanical apparatus handed out in the name of Christianity to a bleak world that needs far more the inspiration from a lovely, living, colorful display of flowers. Particularly when those blooms would be a variety called the Rose of Sharon.

Many men are great intellectualizers and tinkerers. Being such must provide strokes to the ego. We have come to think that we must master everything with our minds or hands. We must take things apart to see how they work. Modern man struggles to try and understand absolutely everything. Nothing is sacred, nothing to be approached with a hands-off, walking-on-holy-ground attitude. We speak of *mastering* the puzzle of nature, *cracking* the genetic code, *conquering* outer space. Understanding something with our minds seems to make us feel we somehow triumph over it and subjugate it. This may have its value in science, but it also has its limits when it comes to religion. It can quickly lead to the sorry state of knowing much, but understanding little. When Johnny is found howling in the middle of the kitchen floor on Christmas morning with pieces of his new red fire engine scattered about, he may be in the position of knowing more about his toy than before, but certainly he is not able to enjoy it as much. That primal howl still echoes down from the Garden of Eden where man determined to gain knowledge outside of God's order. He has yet to put back together what he has broken and scattered to the four corners of the world.

The things of God, then, are more affairs of the heart than the head. It is not that the Father does not wish us to get deeply into them, for indeed He does; but they are more to be experienced than conceptualized. It is more a matter of walking quietly hand in hand with God in the garden at the end of the day and learning from His very presence instead of slyly biting into the apple when no one is looking to learn what its effects are.

The kingdom of God is a kingdom of faith, and not of reason alone. He who pursues it with the intellect alone will *never* find it. Its foundation principle and ultimate end is not some cleverly hidden mystery; it is unselfish love. This kingdom can never be attained by the workings of the most profound intellect. It is not something the most diligent pursuit of logic is able to lead one to possess or experience.

Men's great needs are devotional, not theological. A Christianity centered in the person of God is vital, not a socially-centered or a church-centered or a truth-centered or even a Bible-centered religion. Certainly the Bible is precious, for it can lead a man to God. But remember, the Good Book is the *love letter*, not the *marriage*. One can know the Book well without knowing and loving the Author. The Bible is not to be worshiped. God is. "The knowledge of God," said Blaise Pascal, "is very far from the love of Him."

The true believer will devote himself to becoming an

expert at worshiping, praising, and experiencing the living God. He will not limit the advancement of his spiritual life to acquiring additional religious or theological facts and insights. Instead he will joyously throw himself with total abandon into tasting and experiencing within his own heart and soul the inner sweetness of the very nature of God. *We scientifically-oriented, intellect-worshiping, space-age Christians need nothing quite so badly as to keep our theology more simple and our love more profound!*

Are those with the keenest memories and highest IQs the surest candidates to qualify for the kingdom of God? The truth comes ringing down from Calvary that men are saved by faith, not knowledge. Faith is many more parts love than learning. It is much more a product of trust than of reasoning. "Look, love, and live," says Scripture.

Two very unique books in the Old Testament, found side by side, were written by the same author. One, Ecclesiastes, speaks of the way of wisdom, the other, The Song of Songs, speaks of the way of love. Unless Ecclesiastes is read with the full intent of the writer in mind, it can be a very depressing book. It is a picture of man trying to work out with reason alone the great issues of life and death and God. One of its most profound concepts is the limitation and the ultimate futility of human wisdom. To "search out by wisdom concerning all things that are done under heaven" leads Solomon to the tragic conclusion again and again that "all is vanity," or emptiness.[1] "For in much wisdom is much grief: and he that increaseth knowledge increaseth sorrow."[2] In fact, he goes on to associate the building up of the intellect alone and the pursuit of wisdom merely for wisdom's sake with eventual madness![3] History has proven him correct.

Whenever man has attempted to divorce his intellect from his soul, whenever he has enthroned his mind over his heart, he has begun the journey toward madness and despair. Nazism provides a perfect example. "Wisdom" took precedence over conscience. If something appeared logical and expedient, it became right, and it dictated the course of action. "Might makes right" was the theme. Whatever contributed to the development of the "master race" was good. Today we look back with shock and horror at the completely unbelievable events that philosophy engendered. It has come to be called "the holocaust."

Nor can logic ever explain faith and love. Logic has its own way of always coming full circle and meeting its own end when pursued long enough. Logic is a god that has always proven to be too small. To depend on human reasoning ability alone is an invitation to disaster, whether that reasoning ability is made the ultimate end of anything from the social to the political to the religious.

Only if men were to take the intellect and its favorite heir apparent—science—off earth's throne and replace it with the divine principle of unselfish love would this world ever become a paradise instead of a hell. Since God knows this could never happen, He has had to intervene and break the bewitching spell cast in Eden. He will prevent the ultimate holocaust. He will bring in His kingdom just in time to keep all humankind from vanishing into the abyss it has dug for itself with its "wisdom."

What intelligent, knowledgeable American would not agree that "wisdom" dictates a defense budget in this country of billions of dollars? Our best minds and facilities are dedicated to developing more deadly weapons of destruction. We've come a long way. We even have our clever little neutron bomb now that can evaporate people and leave more "strategically important" things like buildings and bridges intact!

While we are investing our best energy and talent and a great portion of our financial strength in such pursuits, the cancer wards still echo with screams of anguish. Mothers on the other side of the world clutch bony children to their breasts who are daily dying for the want of a five-cent cup of milk. But it is *reasonable* to maintain our defense priorities, to protect ourselves, wouldn't you say? The answer is that somehow a situation has been created where it is reasonable and logical and necessary to do what is counterproductive and mindless and insane! Human wisdom has lead us full circle again. We have become the victims of believing in our own minds. There is always going to be that point where, though it looks so promising at first, the ultimate end of the pursuit of wisdom for wisdom's sake will be hopelessness, insanity, and despair.

The degree of trust and confidence mistakenly placed in human wisdom is appalling. Even more appalling is the veneration with which some Christians regard religious knowledge and theological learning and the readiness they exhibit to center their spiritual lives around it instead of around a relationship of personal oneness with a loving God.

Too many believers are running around trying to be "Christian scientists." They seem to think that with the proper amount of study and understanding and intellectual insight or biblical knowledge they can attain true spirituality.

Dependence on and the enshrinement of his own powerful intellect is what felled Lucifer, chief angel of heaven! Pursuing logic ahead of commitment to God is what led to the first sin by Adam and Eve. It was just not *logical* that the fruit of one tree, as beautiful as all the others, could not be sampled! There was a good reason God called the tree which led to their fall "the tree of knowledge of good and evil." Elevating the pursuit of knowledge above a personal relationship with God is what brought war in heaven and despair and death to the paradise of earth.

Ever since the fall, the intellect has been an idol which is like a black hole that pulls men and women into an abyss of no return. That void is well-nigh plugged today with a rush of countless eager, well-meaning individuals whose worship of reason has led them to attempt to outthink God. This is just what the splendid angel Lucifer did, the one who ended up a devil.

Realizing the inadequacy of reason, Malcom Muggeridge wrote: "I do not think that the intellect, reason, can produce an answer to life, and I don't know of any person for whom I have any respect, including many scientists, among them the greatest, who has not seen that reason is an inadequate instrument, and that one can only appreciate what life is about through this other dimension which we call faith."[4]

So, fellow seeker, if you wish the knowledge of good and evil, if you want to know the realities of life and death and of Almighty God, if you value sagacity and crave the precious pearls of spiritual wisdom and long to explore the distant dimensions of truth, you dare not pursue your quest with the vehicle of your own intellect alone.

If it is wisdom you desire, learn well this lesson: *You will discern the truth of God only by becoming a partaker of God's divine nature*. As you and I practice the presence of the living God and draw into close, conscious awareness of Him daily, we will come to know the truth. "I am . . . the truth," said Jesus.[5] If you would know the truth, then come to know Him. Intimately. Let His very self be formed within your mind and heart. The center of spirituality, the inmost glory of the gospel, is not a great doctrine or a great message or a great movement, but a great Person. It is Jesus Christ Himself. He did not come so much to proclaim a message as to insure that there would be a message to proclaim. His remedy for a lost world was not a new system of teaching, but Himself. Not a body of doctrine, but Himself. To be a Christian then is to enter constantly into a relationship with this Person. This Person who walks with you as a friend, who communes with you, who shares His own eternal life with you.

How sad that many have been deluded into regarding Christianity as a devout intellectual exercise or the subscription to certain religious beliefs or the acquiring of ecclesiastical knowledge.

Multitudes are focusing on their own reasoning ability or relying on pastors or priests or scholars to infuse them with spirituality and interpret truth for them. A great number of devoutly religious people have simply lost sight of the real meaning of Christianity. They have lost sight of a friendship with Christ. They need to direct their eyes to His divine Person, His marvelous merits, His endless, changeless, unconditional love. "Look unto me, and be ye saved, all the ends of the earth."[6]

Remember the time the children of Israel were attacked by poisonous serpents in the wilderness? God instructed Moses to hold up a brass serpent on a pole for all to see so that those who looked at it might be spared. Some said, "Well now, that makes no sense at all. It is not logical that viewing a metal serpent on a rod will do anything to counteract snake venom!"

Those who philosophized or argued or expected an explanation, feeling they had to understand it all before it could do them any good, soon died in agony. Those who in simple trust and faith turned their gaze on what was a symbol of Christ were spared. Those who looked, lived.

If you feel you have to have everything completely explained to you, if you believe you have to reason out every point and comprehend every facet of the walk with God, if you wait until you can grasp every doctrine with your intellect before you begin your intimate, daily walk with him, you are in as much danger of dying in your sins as those analytical Hebrews of dying of snakebite.

For those who simply trust in a personal love relationship with God to save them, no proof is necessary. For those who must have everything proven to them first, no proof is possible. This is true not only of eternal life, but of receiving any good gift from God, including the special experience of enjoying oneness with God and the transfusion of the very nature of Christ into you right now.

Every believer must discover that many of the dimensions of the spiritual life are beyond human logic. The Bible speaks of a God "which doeth great things past finding out."[7] When Jesus' disciples wanted to delve into some of the most profound elements of truth while they ignored far more important matters in their own relationships, He said to them, "I have yet many things to say unto you, but ye cannot bear them now."[8]

Later when Peter insisted on being informed about something that should have been no concern of his, Jesus rebuked, "What is that to thee? follow thou me."[9]

"Follow thou me"—words everyone needs to hear

when they attempt to put anything but Christ at the center stage of their minds.

I do not wish to disparage formal religious scholarship in this chapter. It is valuable and has its place. It simply must never be confused for a moment with living Christianity. It must never be substituted for the way of love and oneness as the path to the holy of holies, to the heart of God, to life eternal. It is hard not to appreciate the point of the evangelist Billy Sunday when he exclaimed, "I don't know any more about theology than a jackrabbit does about ping-pong, but I am on my way to glory!"

Formal religious learning is primarily an intellectual exercise. While believers may benefit from it, they also need to be wary of the wrong directions it can lead. A reminder of such dangers came recently when the Associated Press carried a quote from one well-known theologian in newspapers across the country. This gentleman, who has a doctorate in religion, was lamenting how difficult it was for the laymen in his denomination to comprehend an issue that was dividing their church. "Biblical studies," he said, "have advanced to a place of highly specialized skills. Basically, what we have now is the old 'town versus gown' problem. When people without specialized training try to do theology, it's about the same as if people who don't know electronics were put in charge of NASA."[10]

Any church which has "progressed" to the point where the average person in the pews can no longer grasp the basic truths of its teaching is in serious danger of falling into the same trap as Lucifer—trying to outthink and outexplain God.

To the horror of some believers today the medieval church in Europe taught that only the clergy were educated and inspired enough to understand and interpret the Scriptures. The average person was not even allowed to own a Bible. While it is obvious that this thinking was wrong, it is not so obvious that we are in danger of having come full circle today. Our fascination with professional religious wisdom-seeking and the quest for intellectual religious knowledge—often for the sake of satisfying the intellect and, all too often, the ego of the searcher—has brought us squarely to the point where the emphasis now on understanding spiritual things and on interpreting the Bible is placed on intellectual skills and acquired scholastic training. By not relying primarily on the Holy Spirit living in the soul of the believer as the guide and source of insight and inspiration in interpreting the Scriptures, many are falling into something resembling the old medieval trap.

Satan is earth's most proficient theologian. He has applied masterful intellect to advancing His wisdom for millenia. He knows more facts about God; he has more knowledge of religious truth than the most dedicated human scholar who has ever lived. But he is the devil. His keenest, most expansive insight would not be worth trading for one moment's worth of reverent oneness with God, which the humblest believer may continually enjoy.

Many preachers and Bible scholars need to learn today that the clearest, most logical proclamation of even the finest truths is worthless unless it carries the hearers beyond intellectual comprehension into a personal experience with God.

Jesus built no altars to religious scholarship. Indeed some of His most determined enemies—such as Saul of Tarsus—came from such ranks. Instead He made some intriguing statements that reflect a whole different system of simple spiritual values. "I thank thee, O

Father, Lord of heaven and earth," Christ could pray, "because thou hast hid these things from the wise and prudent, and hast revealed them unto babes."[11]

He cautioned those among His listeners who took pride in their wisdom and learning, "Whosoever shall not receive the kingdom of God as a little child, he shall not enter therein."[12]

This statement enraged the rabbis and Pharisees in the audience who had conned the worshipers into measuring their spiritual leaders' piety and devotion by the extent of the knowledge they had of religious and scriptural topics.

Jesus was saying, If you people want a spiritual hero, do not look to Caiaphas or some temple rabbi. If you want to find the way to the heart of God, look into the face of a little child. You will get better answers there than from any textbook or gathering of eminent divines.

It is certainly the unpretensiousness, the simplicity, and the self-forgetfulness of a small child that led Christ to commend children's attitudes as the appropriate method of drawing close to God. Most importantly a child responds to someone from the heart, not from the intellect. The self-confiding love of a little child, offered in simple trust, is the best pattern you can use in developing a relationship, a closeness with God.

The Christian religion did not have its beginning among brilliant, academic minds or among the rich and powerful. It grew from the spontaneous response of some unaffected, uncomplicated, unassuming simple-hearted people. They were drawn, like the compulsion of a moth to the flame, to the extraordinary love and sensitivity of the life Jesus Christ was showing in the world.

These were men who made what appeared to be very irrational, illogical decisions, such as walking away from their boats, their secure government jobs, their homes and friends. Some thought their behavior was almost childish! Running off after some itinerant preacher! "And he saith unto them, Follow me, and I will make you fishers of men. And they straightway left their nets, and followed him. . . . And they immediately left the ship and their father, and followed him."[13] These men responded to the tugging at their hearts, not to a series of facts presented to their heads. Love's voice echoed in their souls. They answered in childlike eagerness. Instantly.

"But the best part of the fishing season is just ahead!" their friends may have argued. But they did not even take the time to dry their nets. "What fools!" said the other fishermen. "What love!" said God. And He built His church on these "impulsive" fellows, men who were not afraid to respond to love.

When Solomon wrote Ecclesiastes he showed the futility of attempting to achieve spiritual life through knowledge alone. In his next book, the Song of Songs, he reveals that at last he had learned what his father, David, the man after God's own heart, had learned so well: One can come to know God and His ways only through love.

Scholars of various kinds and persuasions have been puzzled over the Song of Songs for centuries. Some have seen it as being just a sentimental love poem; some have considered it pornography which does not belong in the Bible. It is impossible for those who would understand it only on an intellectual level to get out of it its deep symbolic meaning. But to the believer who sees intimacy with God as the ultimate ground of spiritual being, the book is a source of wonder and exquisite delight. It compares the depth of spiritual affection the Christian is to seek with God to the intimate, passionate, all-engrossing, logically unexplainable desire a bride and groom have for each other emotionally and physically. Such love, of course, rises from deep within the heart and soul. It far surpasses anything that the intellectual thought processes can conceive.

The Song's two lovers experience agony when they are separated. The essense of their existence is for them to be together. They live to experience each other in every dimension. A similar kind of intense, burning spiritual ardor God would have the Christian enjoy with Him. He wants all to understand that such is the very heart of spiritual life.

"His banner over me was love,"[14] the ecstatic bride of the Song declares of her spouse.

Christians must be careful lest they find themselves rallying under the flag of profound thought or elevated intellect, talent, genius, or scholarly knowledge. These things have their value, but they dare not be allowed to supplant the one glorious center for the life devoted to God—the heart that ardently reaches up to heaven in a simple, childlike response—to love.

"That Christ may dwell in your hearts by faith; that ye, being rooted and grounded in love, may be able to comprehend with all saints what is the breadth, and length, and depth, and height; *and to know the love of Christ, which passeth knowledge, that ye might be filled with all the fulness of God.*"[15]

8
To Learn to Ask

And I say unto you, Ask, and it shall be given you. Luke 11:9.

Seven and a half miles from Jerusalem to Emmaus. Cleopas and his friend had made the same journey many times before. But this time they forgot the miles and ups and downs of the road. They were caught up in deep discussion of the amazing events they had witnessed in the preceding two days. They had chosen to be Christ's disciples, and now He had been crucified. They had been so sure that He was going to save Israel, and now their best hopes seemed frustrated. But there was the puzzling report of the women who had visited the tomb. Empty, they said. And they had some sort of vision of angels. Angels telling them He was alive.

The two were so absorbed in their discussion that they scarcely noticed when a man drew alongside and began to keep pace with them. As is so often the case with those caught up in their own affairs they paid the stranger little heed. They did not even speak to Him until He showed His concern and sensitivity by eventually interjecting, "What manner of communications are these that ye have one to another, as ye walk, and are sad?"[1] Cleopas revealed his agitated state of mind over the recent events by his curt reply: Where have you been, man? You must have had your head in the sand if you don't know the things that have been going on in Jerusalem these last few days!

Remarkably the stranger took no offense, but only asked gently, "What things?"[2] In response, touched now by His kindliness and His interest in them, the two began pouring out their hearts. They spoke of their now wavering faith that Jesus was the Messiah. "We trusted that it had been he which should have redeemed Israel: and besides all this, today is the third day since these things were done."[3]

Three days since they had seen their Lord humiliated and crucified. Three days and they had allowed their minds to get so caught up in the turmoil that they were now engrossed in fretting and worrying and doubting. So soon they forgot the most important lessons their Master had taught them—to stay in tune with God, to practice oneness with Him, to take time daily to commune with Him, to turn to His Word for guidance.

Now it was the Stranger's turn to rebuke them. "O fools, and slow of heart to believe," He began, startling them out of their self-pity.[4] Then He gave them a marvelous exposition from the Scriptures. Beginning with the writings of Moses, the Traveler ranged throughout the works of all the prophets that revealed the Messiah. He showed the two how all that had happened to Christ had been foretold. The tragic events of the past week need not cause any doubt that Jesus was the Son of God. They were, in fact, the distinctive, confirming proof that He most certainly was.

Christ did not write with His finger in the sky or cause the rocks to speak out to impress His hearers with the truth. He used the Scriptures, just as they could. So must we first find the truth of God in His Word before we can fully experience His presence in our hearts.

It is the Bible that opens the door to oneness. It is the great disclosure of God Himself and His love for us. Christ comes to men in the garment of Scripture. There is absolutely no substitute for Bible reading for the believer who seriously seeks oneness. To be intimate with God you must associate yourself with His Word daily. Type it on a 3 x 5 card and tape it to your refrigerator or above your desk. Listen to it on tapes as you drive to work. Sing its words to music. Read it to your children at night. Memorize it, assimilate it, meditate on it. Let its precious words integrate themselves into your very soul until they are the flesh and blood of your thinking and living.

A respected minister was conducting a Week of Spiritual Emphasis at a large medical school. A young doctor-in-training came to him one evening for some counsel. "Pastor," he said, "I feel like my spiritual life is slipping away. I just don't have much time for it. Can you give me a prescription that will give me some new life spiritually? I don't want to hear the old routine about taking time for Bible study and prayer and that sort of thing. There must be something else I can do."

"Doctor," said the minister, "I haven't been feeling very energetic lately. I am just not as healthy as I used to be. Can you tell me how I can feel better? I don't want to hear any of that old routine about eating right and exercising every day. I don't have time for that."

As the trio approached the outskirts of Emmaus the Stranger concluded His explanation of the Scripture. The two disciples once again had burning hearts. They were brimming with joy and hope. The two and a half hours spent walking with their companion had endowed them with a new light and life.

As they came near their dwelling in the village the traveler politely made it apparent He was intending to continue on. Cleopas and the other disciple invited Him to lodge with them for the night. It would have been easy to have overlooked this act of hospitality, for they still had much on their minds and they still knew very little about this man Himself. Since it was toward evening and the roads were none too safe from highwaymen after dark, the disciples urged their new Friend to accept their offer, in spite of His making it clear He did not want to force His presence on them. When it was obvious they sincerely wanted Him to stay, "he went in to tarry with them."[5]

So by this simple, sincere request the stage was set for one of the most extraordinary events that ever occurred in the lives of these two men. When they sat down at the table to share a meal with their guest, He was revealed to them as their beloved Saviour!

Christ lived again! Death was conquered! And they were some of the first among men to have seen the resurrected Lord!

After He disappeared, they scrambled hastily to their feet, leaving the rest of the meal unfinished. Heedless of the dark and dangers they hurriedly retraced the seven and a half miles to Jerusalem to share the outstanding news with the other believers.

But what if they had not asked Him in to dwell with them? Their Companion on the road would have been eventually forgotten as just another traveler. His exposition of Scripture would have been remembered as just another opinion. Their faith would have dissolved in the acid of their doubts. Their dreams of a Saviour would have withered away. Their hope evaporated.

Their eternal life, perhaps lost.

But they asked Him in!

And that made all the difference!

Christ's exposition of Scripture informed them, inspired them, and prepared them for a deeper revelation. But it was only when they persistently asked Him in to dwell with them that these men actually saw Him as their Saviour.

To invite the Saviour into the innermost parts of your being is to step through the veil into the holy of holies. It is to be transformed by a new and splendid vision from the clouded world of the material and physical to the genuine insight, truth, and reality of the spiritual.

To see with only your own vision, your own reason, your own intellect is to see only another Stranger. To see after you have put on the "glasses" of the Holy Spirit is to see God and to know Him as your own Father.

You need only ask. *Concentrate whatever willpower you have in the direction of knowing Jesus and allowing Him to dwell in you, and you will have found the great and simple key to unlocking the limitless storehouses of heaven and eternity.*

On every walk the same Stranger that joined the two on the way to Emmaus is waiting to accompany you. He wishes to open your eyes to the marvels of who He is and what He can do in your life. He wants you to go out with joy, carrying a message to the world like the disciples did. There is a Saviour! He is risen! Death is conquered! Life and love have meaning!

But in order to appropriate these truths into your own life you must first ask Him in.

More than anything else Christianity is a matter of asking. And continuing to ask. If you are not experiencing the closeness with God your heart cries for, the reason is that you are not asking. Victory is in the asking. The Bible says simply, "Ye have not, because ye ask not."[6]

The main difference between Christians and non-Christians is that Christians are continual askers and promise claimers. And that makes all the difference. "Whereby are given unto us exceeding great and precious promises: *that by these ye might be partakers of the divine nature.*" Or, as the New English Bible puts it, "Through this might and splendour he has given us his promises, great beyond all price, and through them you may escape the corruption with which lust has infected the world, *and come to share in the very being of God.*"[7]

In His story of the importunate neighbor, Jesus showed that in order to receive any spiritual promise, one must persistently ask for it. The man got his loaves of bread to feed his guest only because he persistently knocked on the door and kept asking for them.

God does not lightly bestow any of His spiritual treasures. The most valuable of them all, the gift of His personal presence dwelling in the believer through the filling of the Holy Spirit, is available to everyone. Everyone, that is, who cares enough for it to keep on asking. It is the faithful, persistent, even tenacious asking that reveals the Christian's sincere desire to receive God's favors. It separates the genuine, passionate desire from the shallow, trifling request.

If you really want oneness with God, you must possess the same boldness Jacob did when he stubbornly clung to the mighty Angel through the night, insisting on His blessing before he would release Him.

In telling specifically how one may acquire the intimate unity with God the Holy Spirit provides, Jesus said plainly, "Ask, and it shall be given you; seek, and ye shall find; knock, and it shall be opened. . . . If ye then being evil, know how to give good gifts unto your children: how much more shall your heavenly Father give the Holy Spirit to them that ask him?"[8]

In this book the tremendous importance of centering one's spiritual life around intimacy with God has received most of the attention. It would be unfair, however, not to explore with the reader the *way* of attaining this intimacy. It would also be unfair to suggest that it best becomes a reality by any other means than asking for the filling of the Holy Spirit.*

Jesus was actually excited that He could leave earth. When His mission was done He was intensely anxious to have His work in the world replaced by that of the Spirit, for He knew what this could mean to the human race.

Some marvel that Christ's ministry on earth was so very short, just three and a half years. Since He was such a blessing to mankind, since it was such a miracle for Him to even be here, and since He healed so many and preached truth so distinctly, why, they reason, could He not stay longer? Why not a lifetime with us?

But His brief stay should not puzzle us. In fact, we should perhaps wonder why His ministry was not far shorter. He came to accomplish a specific task. When He laid down His life, He provided two great gifts to me; (1) eternal life and (2) the right to oneness again with God.

Sinlessness is not an end in itself. It is not, contrary to popular religious opinion, the ultimate spiritual experience. *It is very important because it is the condition needed for intimacy with God.* Christ's greatest

*In the author's *Living in Our Finest Hour* (Mountain View, Calif.: Pacific Press Publishing Association, 1982) he covers the filling of the Spirit in detail.

accomplishment was to open the way for men to come back into unity and harmony and intimacy with God.

If we Christians only claim half His work for us, if we seek only forgiveness and eternal life and do not care enough to aggressively pursue and persistently ask for the great dimension of oneness with God, we blaspheme the very death of Christ on the cross.

We are too often like the little child at Christmas who receives a valuable gift but throws it aside and plays with the cardboard box it came in.

Jesus yearned for the greatest payoff from His sacrifice to be implemented. He had accomplished His mission, had won eternal life for us. Then He departed for heaven so that the next miraculous, vitally important phase could be implemented by heavenly command—the indwelling of the lives of people with the very presence of God through the ministry of the Holy Spirit. This ministry transforms the nature of men and women into the nature of God. This transforming gives the gift of eternal life its best meaning and its ultimate fulfillment.

If living forever was the only gift from heaven, Jesus could just as well have stayed on earth after His resurrection to help the apostles take this good news to the world. But He returned to heaven so that the other great prize He won for humanity could be implemented. Because of the limitations He assumed when He took human nature, He could not personally administer the indwelling of God within men. "Nevertheless I tell you the truth," He said. "It is expedient for you that I go away: for if I go not away, the Comforter will not come unto you; but if I depart, I will send him unto you."[9]

After His resurrection Christ burned with desire to make the Holy Spirit available to men as quicky as possible. He longed for them to experience the same closeness with their heavenly Father that He enjoyed. He wished more than anything for men to be restored to their original position as reflectors of the image and glory of God, their bodies becoming the very "temple of the Holy Ghost."[10]

"And I will pray the Father," He explained, "and he shall give you another Comforter, that he may abide with you for ever; even the Spirit of truth; whom the world cannot receive, because it seeth him not, neither knoweth him: but ye know him; *for he dwelleth with you, and shall be in you.*"[11]

God living in men again at last! If Jesus had stayed on earth there would have been just one God-man to share the love and the truth of the heavenly kingdom. But with the coming of the omnipresent Spirit *every* believer could begin to have the divine nature developed within himself. There could be many sons of God on earth!

The invitation still stands. The door into the holiest remains open. You and I may enter as we ask for the promised filling of the Holy Spirit.

"That which is conceived in her is of the Holy Ghost," said the angel of the miracle that occurred when Jesus Christ was formed physically within Mary.[12] So also is the life and nature of God formed within the believer today by the sincere, consistent request for the Comforter.

The greatest act of the Spirit in behalf of people is not to prompt prophecies or trigger unknown tongues, but to generate the very love and presence of God in the human heart, to make men into sons of God, to set them ablaze with a power and a passion in their lives that nothing this side of heaven can equal. It is to make them like Jesus—experts at loving and full of joy.

This then is heaven's best offer.

Yours for the asking.

9
To Become Like Him

But of him are ye in Christ Jesus, who of God is made unto us . . . sanctification. 1 Corinthians 1:30.

A skilled craftsman was chiseling a piece of stone at the base of a very tall church. Pointing upward to the top of the sweeping spire, he explained, "See that little opening up there? I am shaping this down here so it will fit up there."

That same thing is exactly what God wants to do with Christians right now. Jesus is sitting for His portrait in every believer. The process of modification will not be totally completed in this life, but it is God's intention to go as far as possible with each one of us before death.

To be a Christian, then, is to be constantly in a state of dynamic metamorphosis. I am not talking about bettering yourself. I am not talking about reading popular self-help manuals or being your own psychologist. I am not talking about improvement. I am talking about *transformation*.

In this book we have been walking on holy ground. We have been discussing intimacy with divinity, oneness with the very mind and person of God. He is the same God who created all of the matter and energy of earth and the universe by His spoken word, the God who ignited the nuclear furnaces of a trillion trillion suns and causes their solar winds to blow. Intense, continuous communion with such a dynamic Being holds potential for nothing short of the believer's transfiguration. Through close, personal fellowship with Him, you may come to share the very life, the very love, the very joy, the very power, and yes, the very eternity of God Almighty. Fellowship with divinity must be seen for what it is, a shaking, shocking, sensational, transforming experience.

By beholding we become changed. This is most true when God is the focus of attention. It is certainly true that you become more and more like whatever you give your time and concentration to. By daily practicing the presence of God, you become remarkably remade into His likeness. Practice is, in fact, the only way to reach this goal. Association with divinity changes ordinary people into extraordinary personalities!

When the mind of man is brought into communion with the mind of God, the mortal with the immortal, the finite with the infinite, the impact on a person is incredible. In such fellowship is the wellspring of life, the grandest source of inspiration, the highest form of education, the greatest motivation for unselfish love.

The practice of oneness with God elevates and ennobles the mind, refines the tastes, and softens and subdues the heart, bringing one into harmony with the will and law of God.

Some would use fear or guilt as the great motive for good behavior. But as a shield from temptation, as an animating force toward decency, purity, and genuine love, nothing can possibly compare with living in the sense of God's presence.

Many mistakenly assume that the believer must constantly struggle to keep from sinning. This is not so. The struggle involves taking time to behold the Saviour. If you wish to enter heaven someday and look on God in all His power and glory, you must become accustomed to focusing on Him, to beholding Him with the eye of faith in the inner consciousness of your mind here and now.

Real transformation into the image of God comes not through trying but abiding, not struggling but beholding. The ultimate experience in Christianity is not to be able to say, "I am living without sin," but, "It is no longer I who live, but Christ who lives in me."[1]

Not even to "imitate" Christ is the believer called. Transformation comes not from simply taking Jesus as an example or role model, not even very studiously trying to behave like Him. Those who never get beyond the spiritual copycat stage are in danger of becoming part of that group who at Christ's return may find themselves crying, "Lord, Lord, have we not prophesied in thy name? and in thy name have cast out devils? and in thy name done many wonderful works?" The Master's tragic response is, "I never *knew* you: depart from me."[2]

Subscribing to a Christian code of ethics, attempting to behave like Jesus, failed to make these people the Lord's. Their one tragic mistake was failing to take time to come to *know* God intimately. These sincere, well-intentioned individuals always found too much to do on the outside to have time to enter into the holy of holies. They lived their spiritual lives in the outer circle of the temple, preoccupied totally with good works or the social melee. They were courtyard Christians who never found the time or inclination to step through the torn veil and look directly into the face of God. They did not make beholding Him the focus of their lives. In spite of their efforts, they were never able to become like Him and could never understand why not. They had such sincerity, such good intentions, such an expenditure of effort and enthusiasm. But they missed everything because they missed intimacy with God.

Always there are two extremes. Others never come into true communion with God because they cannot get past the idea that the spiritual life is some sort of mystical, gossamer, religious fantasyland. But Christianity is the ultimate reality. It is love with skin on it. It is salty tears shed over a dying child or a dying city. It is good, red, human blood, spattered on an olivewood cross with iron spikes in it. Blood containing Mary's chromosomes. But blood without which there would have been no remission for sins. Christianity is the Lord God from heaven come down to walk in the garden in the cool of the day, come to walk among the rhododendron bushes. His great heart even then yearned for friendship and communion with the fearful man and woman who hid there, their naked bodies pressed against the rich dark soil.

It is the devil destined for hell who pictures Christianity as nothing more than an ethereal philosophy for mental subscription. He is Satan, father of the idea that God is some sort of vague spirit cloistered away in celestial tabernacles, remote, taking only the most general interest in the affairs of men. So unapproachable is the Father, says Satan, that believers can draw close to Him only by the most excruciating of spiritual struggles or only after expending the utmost energy to completely purify themselves.

Satan leads people to believe that a relationship with God need make no difference in the way they live. And if they acknowledge God but remain distant and aloof enough from Him to prevent any change in their lives

Satan is certainly more than delighted.

Christ came to show men that the secret to a genuine spiritual life is not in centering one's religious interests around the law or ecclesiastical philosophy or ecclesiastical activities, but around God Himself. Jesus' most important example to men was that they should maintain a constant, ongoing intimacy with God. He demonstrated again and again the significance of continual fellowship with the Father. A sense of God's presence and perfection was always before Him. His life shows more clearly than anything else the world has ever seen the marvelous effect of living close to the heart of God. Having laid aside His own divine nature, He depended solely on oneness with the Father to sustain His spiritual life, just as you and I may do. The result was that His human nature manifested the character of the divine. He showed us what ours can begin to resemble as we too move into genuine fellowship with the Father.

Jesus was patient and calm no matter what occurred. He never became discouraged, ruffled, or fretful. He was the most approachable of men, but He retained a quiet dignity. He was never unduly elated by the applause of His friends or threatened or intimidated by the curses of His enemies. He was no vacant-eyed, mystical philosopher. Shepherds identified with Him. And fishermen. He was an intensely practical Person who could make flawless baby cribs and dining-table chairs.

Jesus enjoyed people. All sorts. Not because He planned it that way, but because of His divine charisma, any group, any party, or any gathering eventually ended up centered around Him.

With the incredible truth He had, with His insights and wisdom, we might have expected Him to have spent most of His time writing and lecturing. But the only writing of His ever recorded He traced with His finger in street-side sand soon destroyed by the feet of the multitude. He spent far more time *healing* than writing or even preaching.

He was a "toucher"—always reaching out to brush the cheek of a little child or to restore sight to blind eyes. It says in the Bible that He "went about doing good."[3]

There are altogether too many people who merely *talk about* being Christians. To represent Christ believers must not only talk but *live* their religion. A Christianity that does not make you like Jesus, a Christianity that does not make you a better person, is no Christanity.

The greatest tragedy of modern times may be that the world is able to see so little of the power of Christianity in Christians. Especially is this true today as the age nears it climax. Shouldn't believers be wildly discontented with religious mediocrity?

The spiritual good must make way for the spiritual best. *The true Christian will accept no lower standard than the perfect life of Jesus Christ!* Such a standard will have the most profound effect on one's actions, one's speech, one's character, one's personality.

God wants His people to be a saving, redemptive force on this planet. Only through practicing oneness with Him can they ever envision and achieve all that He wants. Through the provision of Christ and the indwelling of the Holy Spirit, *man can, when he unites himself with divinity, work the works of God.*

Do you realize that after the Spirit filled the disciples, they did every miracle that Jesus had done? They healed the sick. They cast out demons. They even raised the dead.

God has set no limit on the great and good things believers may do. Your only limit is the degree of closeness you practice with God. Oneness with God brings every believer greatness. Not the greatness of money or power or prestige. But greatness of character, greatness of compassion. Greatness of service and greatness of kindness and greatness of love. When a sinful, selfish human being, by placing himself close to the heart of God, takes on these characteristics, this is divinity working in humanity. This is the most wonderful of miracles.

We have only just begun to tap the resources of heaven. We have only just begun to become like the Master, to show His works in the world, to reveal His love. The greatest hymns are yet to be composed. The most beautiful, uplifting music is yet to be sung. The finest books are yet to be written. The greatest acts of mercy and compassion are yet to be performed. The best solutions to earth's increasingly frustrating and fearful problems are yet to be devised.

It can be Christians who do these things. It can be Christians who make the greatest contributions. After all, when we come close to God, He lends us His reasoning, and we become most wise. He lends us His love, and we become most loving.

It is almost a game today for some believers to see how close they can come to the world and still remain Christians. Why don't we start making it popular for believers to concentrate on becoming as much like Christ as they can?

Those who do choose to go all out with intimacy with God soon lose the natural inclination to settle for mediocrity. They become pioneer people. Creative people. Each tomorrow becomes an opportunity to be anticipated.

The church father Irenaeus once wrote, "The glory of God is a man fully alive." Unquestionably, those who practice oneness with God have discovered the essence of living. They are the most productive people in the world.

"He that abideth in me, . . . bringeth forth much fruit," promised Jesus.[4] What is the "much fruit" that you and I can bear? Is it not more than anything else the fruit of a heavenly nature? Is it not the evidence of the power of truth and love in our characters? Is it not the ability to lead a life above reproach? When we not only talk but live our religion, then we show that we are branches of the living Vine.

Speaking of the impact the Holy Spirit living within His followers would have, Jesus said, "He that believeth on me, as the scripture hath said, out of his belly shall flow rivers of living water."[5] Wouldn't you like to be the kind of person who always has something good to give? Whose very presence never fails to prove a blessing and inspiration to others whom your life touches? Wouldn't you like to feel that what you do will account for some great good in the world? Wouldn't you like to feel that there was eternal impact and significance in all your words, all your actions? *By practicing intimacy with God, your life can become one great, ongoing, productive miracle.*

For far too long too many Christians have equated the success of their spiritual lives with how much they have managed to accumulate materially and financially. These things may indeed be symptomatic of God's blessing, but they must never be regarded as a substitute for that which is of far greater value. For, "It is not what we get, but what we give, that measures the worth of the life we live."

Christians should not be sitting around reading good books all the time. They should be writing them. And if they cannot do that they should be out giving them away. Christians should not always be so eagerly watching movies and television. They should be creating more films instead of leaving it largely to the godless to do. Christians should be writing the hit songs. Hosting the talk shows, entertaining the troops, editing the papers, commenting on the day's news. Scouting the frontiers of medical, environmental, and energy research. Not that believers would engage in any of these activities in a strikingly religious way. But the impact of their living in intimacy with God would have a spontaneous crossover into all that they did. They could draw on this limitless source for their wisdom, their inspiration. They could count on it to help them make a distinctly unique contribution.

Where are the Daniels today in the throne rooms of the world? Where are the Josephs in the palaces of the kings? Is it too much to ask for great Christian statesmen to rise again to help guide the world in its most troubled hour?

In all ages the "Spirit of Christ which was in them"[6] has made God's true prophets the light of the people of their generation. Never has there been a time when the problems men face have been as intense as they are today. In the time of greatest darkness more brightly burns the candle.

God calls believers today more than ever before to bring the candle of their lives out from under the bushel of selfish preoccupation and materialism. They are to become the "light of the world, a city that is set on an hill," a candle that "giveth light unto all that are in the house." "Let your light so shine before men, that they may see your good works, and glorify your Father which is in heaven," commanded Jesus.[7]

You have it on the authority of Christ. Good works, when they spring spontaneously from an intimate fellowship with God, form an integral part of the genuine spiritual life.

In the ledgers of evil it is to the devil's everlasting credit that he has devalued the significance of good acts and good behavior in some religious circles. So successful has he been that many consider it blasphemous and anti-gospel even to mention good works. As Satan schemes constantly to convince men they may be saved in their sins, the Bible constantly proclaims that men may be saved *from* their sins.

The believer's highest calling is to let others see God's love through his character and actions. Loving conduct reveals the very purpose of one's existence. The Master has summoned us to a truly remarkable role. Accepted now, this role will continue into eternity, as human beings eventually take the place of angels who fell from God. Redeemed human beings will be the universe's experts in revealing the true nature and character of God. Throughout eternity those who have experienced firsthand His redeeming love, His forgiving mercy, and His transforming power will never tire of revealing the ever-increasing richness of Christ's character in their lives.

What Christians do, say, and are should come to be an expression of the mind of God. When one enters into true oneness with the Father, he will be unable to conceal in his life the light of God's presence.

The love of God is diffusive, aggressive, and totally uncontainable. Its power, glowing in the heart, gives to others a glimpse of heaven. It compels them to appreciate the excellence of the things of God and if they are willing, to be themselves drawn toward the Father.

Those who practice intimacy with God may actually come to be surrounded with a divine atmosphere. Their words, their presence, will warm others in even the most common ways. They will even come to look different physically. They will possess a portion of the same spiritual glow that bathed the face of Moses when he came down from the mountain after communing face-to-face with God.

Oneness with the Father unquestionably lends a vitalness, a force of energy to the believer which of himself he does not possess. This oneness is penetrating. It reaches out and lends inspiration and moral power to others. It attracts all kinds of people to the kingdom of God.

One who comes close to the Father will not want to jeopardize or diminish that special, sweet relationship in any way. Anything that would prevent a person from revealing the Father to another individual will be gladly renounced. Anything that would keep anyone from drawing ever closer to God will be happily discarded. After all, can a dirty mirror fully reflect even the brightest light? God simply cannot manifest Himself through a person whose mind and character are in a wrong condition, a condition that results from purposely practicing sin or intentionally making selfish choices. "Every man that hath this hope in him purifieth himself, even as he is pure."[8]

Rather than struggling to outdistance that swift runner, sin, ride in the chariot with God. Instead of struggling to purify your own soul, rely instead on the natural, refining fire that has its effect only when one encounters the presence of God. Sin and selfishness melt away in the penetrating, transforming warmth of the Father's love. Abiding in God brings purity. Nothing else. "Whosoever abideth in him sinneth not."[9]

Heaven offers the gracious gift of intimacy with the Father to every believer right now. The man or woman who accepts truly enters into another dimension of life.

To practice the presence of God is to come alive spiritually, mentally, and physically. It is to experience a great adventure in personal growth that will continue throughout eternity.

"This world is a great sculptor's shop," C. S. Lewis once said. "We are the statues and there is a rumour going round the shop that some of us are some day going to come to life."[10]

God has been in the business of transforming people ever since Calvary tore down the barriers to the vital power of His presence. You and I do not have to wait until the second coming or the resurrection. We can be infused with His life and experience this ongoing transformation right now. The Christian life now is not some sort of ecclesiastical holding pattern of religious circles the believer maintains until he receives his final clearance to go through the pearly gates. The kingdom of heaven, which is living a godly life, begins whenever anyone enters into fellowship with God through the indwelling of His Holy Spirit. Life becomes a grand and glorious progression toward total oneness and identity with the Father.

Every time one who has such oneness makes a choice he turns into something at least somewhat different. By practicing His presence he slowly becomes a little more like his heavenly Father. Otherwise he drifts ever deeper into selfishness and eternal loneliness, a separation and alienation from one another and from his Father.

God plans to make all human beings into radiant, immortals, splendid reflectors of His love, His joy, His wisdom, and His goodness. I pray, dear reader, that this book has helped you grasp the marvelous vision of what may be. For the Christian's real living has, after all, only just begun.

References

To Enter Within the Veil

1. Exodus 26:31.
2. Mark 15:37, 38.
3. Exodus 40:34.
4. Hebrews 10:19, 20.
5. Ephesians 2:22.
6. Ephesians 2:13.
7. Colossians 1:27.

To Know Him

1. C. S. Lewis, *Mere Christianity* (London: Collings Press, 1955), p. 50.
2. Psalm 42:1, 2.
3. Psalm 63:8.
4. John 5:39, 40, Jerusalem.
5. Revelation 21:2.
6. Genesis 4:25.
7. A. W. Tozer, *The Pursuit of God* (Harrisburg, Penn: Christian Publications Inc., 1948), pp. 10, 13.
8. Mark 1:35; Matthew 14:23.
9. Matthew 6:33.
10. Deuteronomy 4:29.
11. Matthew 7:23.
12. John 17:3.
13. Romans 11:33.
14. Philippians 3:8.

To Be One

1. 2 Corinthians 5:17.
2. Romans 12:2.
3. Matthew 26:26-28.
4. 2 Corinthians 6:16.
5. Philippians 2:5.
6. Romans 12:1.
7. John 12:24, 25.
8. Mark 8:34-36.
9. John 1:12.
10. Matthew 9:3, 5, 6.
11. Luke 2:25, 30, 32.
12. Luke 1:37.
13. Luke 1:38.
14. John 17:22, 23.
15. John 17:14.
16. Lewis, *Mere Christianity*, p. 149.

To Worship Him

1. Psalm 37:4.
2. Robert M. Johnston, "The Devotional Life of Brother Lawrence, *Ministry*, July 1981, p. 22.
3. *Ibid.*
4. *Ibid*, p. 23.
5. 1 Corinthians 10:31.
6. Matthew 18:3.
7. Isaiah 53:6.
8. Johnston, "Brother Lawrence," p. 23.

To Be Blessed

1. *These Times*, April 1981, p. 27.
2. Psalm 91:1.
3. John 21:22.
4. 2 Samuel 8:6.
5. Psalm 84:2.
6. Psalm 107:15.
7. Psalm 42:1.
8. Psalm 9:10.
9. Acts 13:22. (Emphasis supplied.)
10. Genesis 22:18.
11. John 15:5.
12. Genesis 13:2.
13. Psalm 1:3.
14. Luke 7:38.
15. Tozer, *The Pursuit of God*, pp. 19, 20.
16. Genesis 15:1.
17. Deuteronomy 15:18.
18. Deuteronomy 28:3-12.
19. John 15:15.

20. Galatians 3:14.
21. Galatians 3:29.
22. Psalm 37:4.
23. John 15:7. (Emphasis supplied.)
24. Ephesians 3:18, 19.

To Experience Heaven Now

1. Psalm 139:7-10.
2. Psalm 16:11.
3. John 17:3.
4. 2 Corinthians 5:20.
5. John 8:36.
6. Luke 17:21.
7. Colossians 1:13.

To Know the Limits of Reason.

1. Ecclesiastes 1:13, 14.
2. Ecclesiastes 1:18.
3. Ecclesiastes 1:17.
4. Malcolm Muggeridge, *Jesus Rediscovered* (London: Williams Collins and Sons), p. 175.
5. John 14:6.
6. Isaiah 45:22.
7. Job 9:10.
8. John 16:12.
9. John 21:22.
10. *Anchorage Times*, December 27, 1980.
11. Matthew 11:25.
12. Mark 10:15.
13. Matthew 4:19-22.
14. Song of Solomon 2:4.
15. Ephesians 3:17-19. (Emphasis supplied.)

To Learn to Ask

1. Luke 24:17.
2. Luke 24:19.
3. Luke 24:21.
4. Luke 24:25.
5. Luke 24:29.
6. James 4:2.
7. 2 Peter 1:4, KJV, NEB. (Emphasis supplied.)
8. Luke 11:9-13.
9. John 16:7.
10. 1 Corinthians 6:19.
11. John 14:16, 17.
12. Matthew 1:20.

To Become Like Him

1. Galatians 2:20, RSV.
2. Matthew 7:22, 23.
3. Acts 10:38.
4. John 15:5.
5. John 7:38.
6. 1 Peter 1:11.
7. Matthew 5:14-16.
8. 1 John 3:3.
9. 1 John 3:6.
10. Lewis, *Mere Christianity*, p. 136.